THE Jargon
OF Authenticity

THEODOR W. ADORNO

THE Jargon
OF Authenticity

TRANSLATED BY

Knut Tarnowski
and Frederic Will

NORTHWESTERN UNIVERSITY PRESS

Evanston   1973

Copyright © 1973 by Northwestern University Press
Library of Congress Catalog Card Number: 72-96701
ISBN 0-8101-0407-5
Printed in the United States of America
Second printing, 1979
First Paperback Printing, 1983
Second Paperback Printing, 1985
Third Paperback Printing, 1989
The Jargon of Authenticity was originally published
in German under the title *Jargon der Eigentlichkeit:
Zur deutschen Ideologie*. © Suhrkamp Verlag, Frank-
furt am Main, 1964

Knut Tarnowski is an instructor in comparative
literature at the University of Massachusetts.
Frederic Will is professor of comparative literature
at the University of Massachusetts.

CONTENTS

FOREWORD

PHILOSOPHY WHICH ONCE
SEEMED OUTMODED IS NOW
ALIVE BECAUSE THE MOMENT
OF ITS REALIZATION HAS BEEN
MISSED.
Theodor W. Adorno

Existentialism has been de-
scribed by Paul Tillich as "an over one hundred year
old movement of rebellion against the dehumanization
of man in industrial society." [1] But this rebellion has
been viewed as emerging because the solutions pro-
posed by Hegel and Marx proved ineffective for overcoming the fact of alienation.[2] Thus Kierkegaard, in
rejecting Hegel's immanentism of Reason in history
simply tried to restore the irreducibility of human subjectivity. For Kierkegaard the suffering of the individual is not justified in a panlogism of history.

The Jargon of Authenticity is Theodor W. Adorno's

1. Paul Tillich, "Existentialist Philosophy," *The Journal of
the History of Ideas,* V (Jan., 1944), 44–70.
2. F. H. Heinemann, *Existentialism and the Modern Pre-
dicament* (New York, 1958), p. 12.

critique of the ideology of German existentialism. As an expression of the Frankfurt school of critical theory,[3] Adorno's critique is a Hegelian-Marxist response to the existentialist rejection of critical reason. Although this analysis focuses upon twentieth-century German existentialism, especially its post-World War II diffusion, the basic concern is its notion of subjectivity. That is, Adorno's critique is itself an attempt to transcend and include in the perspective of critical reason the truth of the existentialist concern for the fundamentalness of human subjectivity. In this sense Adorno's analysis parallels that of Jean-Paul Sartre, who in the introduction to the *Critique of Dialectical Reason* argues that, correctly understood, existentialism is a moment of dialectical, or critical, reason.[4]

However, Adorno's intent goes beyond a counter-critique of existentialism and aspires to be a critique of the ideology inherent in its German formulations. Adorno not only wants to salvage the notion of subjectivity from the idealistic tendency of existentialism, a concern he shares with Sartre, but he also wants to show that this theory has become a mystification of the actual processes of domination. In this way Adorno's critique is within the tradition of critical theory's critique of ideology. The intent of critical theory is to re-

3. The Frankfurt school is best known by its leading members, among whom are Max Horkheimer, Walter Benjamin, Herbert Marcuse, and Jürgen Habermas. However, these are only the better-known members of a tradition of critical theory that has now spanned two generations. An excellent intellectual history of this highly important and little understood community of radical scholars has just been published by Martin Jay under the title of *The Dialectical Imagination* (Boston, 1973).

4. Jean-Paul Sartre, *Search for a Method* (New York, 1963).

construct the generation of historical forms of consciousness in order to demonstrate how they misrepresent actual social relations and thereby justify historical forms of domination. In this way dialectical reason is actualized by critical theorists who, in their reflective critiques of the basic categories of historical consciousness, seek to reconcile men and women to the actuality of their historical possibilities. So conceived, critical theory is a theoretical moment of the "class struggle."

However, the later Frankfurt school no longer assumed that the categories of Marx's critique of political economy were adequate for the critique of late industrial society (i.e., both "capitalisms" and "socialisms"). It was precisely the failure of Marx's historical agent of change, the proletariat, to become a class-for-itself that stimulated the Frankfurt school's analyses of the ideological reifications that blocked human liberation. Their concern for the growth of false consciousness generated by the "culture industry" and the increased integration, and yet atomization, of persons in the industrial order resulted in a series of critical analyses of mass culture and ideological traditions, e.g., authoritarian social forms, the legacy of the Enlightenment's notion of Reason, etc.[5] In the absence of a decisive agent of social change, and in the midst of what Marcuse termed a "one-dimensional society," the basic interest of the Frankfurt school was to restore the actuality of critical rationality. Indeed, their refusal to affirm "mechanical Marxism" or utopian hopes for

5. Some of these studies are now available in English, such as M. Horkheimer and Theodor W. Adorno, *Dialectic of Enlightenment* (New York, 1972); Max Horkheimer, *Critical Theory* (New York, 1972).

liberation is perhaps evidence of their consistency in staying within the limits of negative critique. For them, only in the negation of pseudo-integrations and resolutions was emancipatory action clearly possible. Hence, the Frankfurt school became a tradition of revolutionary theorists who, in the absence of the objective possibilities for the transcendence of industrial domination, attempted to uphold the ideals of critical reason that anticipated the emancipation of mankind from the unnecessary power constraints of nature and history. In this way their work is basically a critique of the reifications that conceal the truth of critical reason. Since "reification" is for them "a forgetting," [6] their work is essentially a remembrance, from the historical setting of the mid-twentieth century, of the notion of critical reason.

Adorno's *The Jargon of Authenticity* continues the critique of existentialism that had always been an issue for Frankfurt theorists.[7] The continuity of this critique can be shown by Adorno's 1939 essay "On Kierkegaard's Doctrine of Love," which anticipates and is assumed by this book.[8] Adorno shows that Kierkegaard's notion of love transcended human differences, happiness, and even historical morality itself. The

6. Horkheimer and Adorno, *Dialectic of Enlightenment.*
7. Perhaps the earliest statement of this concern is Adorno's *Habilitationsarbeit* (1933), which was published as *Kierkegaard: Konstruktion des Aesthetischen* (Frankfurt, 1965). But the essay by Herbert Marcuse, "Existentialism: Remarks on Jean-Paul Sartre's *L'Etre et le néant*," *Philosophy and Phenomonological Research* VII, no. 3 (March, 1948), is one of the most important critiques of existentialism in the Frankfurt tradition.
8. *Zeitschrift fur Sozialforschung*, VIII (1939), 413–29.

most remote neighbor was to be affirmed as much as the most intimate friend; "preference" was to be overcome, and love as *agapē* was to be experienced in a radical inwardness that transcended the natural inclinations of *eros*. Adorno argues that this love's extreme inwardness conceived of itself as its own ground. Hence, while Kierkegaard's doctrine of love aimed at overcoming the reifications of historical context, it actually became, Adorno claims, a reification that could not be actualized. In oppressing both natural drives and the right of the mind to question, radical inwardness loses love's power of reconciling the antagonism between natural instincts and socially formed selves. In abstract inward love, both historical need and happiness are effectively denied. The real object of this love's "desire" is redemption—which becomes the ultimate reality sought.

Adorno shows that this radical Christian inwardness evades the actuality of secular injustice and inequality. Nonetheless, Kierkegaard is more deeply aware of the transformation of the person in the bourgeois epoch than his contemporaries or his later German existentialist followers. That is, he recognized the mechanisms of industrialization that force men into alienated social patterns and reified communications. But this insight only confirmed Kierkegaard's sense that the progress of civilization was the history of advancing decay and further inclined him to the hatred of "leveling" mechanisms and the rejection of the motives of the bourgeois epoch. Only in the radical inwardness of Christian love, in the leap of faith that suspends the ethical, is it possible to hope for eternality, for redemption.

But Adorno's central point is that Kierkegaard's

radical inwardness has lost the dialectical mediation of subject and object—which was the achievement of Hegel's critical philosophy. That is, the constitutive presuppositions of human subjectivity must themselves be dialectically related to the historical context in which determinate subjects are formed. Failure to so relate the subject and object of historically situated knowledge results in the fallacy of "objectivism"—or the reduction of subjectivity to the in-it-selfness of facts (e.g., positivism) or the innate principles of mind (the idealistic philosophy of the identity of reason and mind). Both forms of objectivism are the loss of critical (dialectical) reason. Only the tradition of reflective critique conceived of human subjectivity in a way that did not reduce it to the determinateness of natural facts or absorb it into the spiritual principles of absolute idealism. Kierkegaard's radical inwardness becomes an idealistic objectivism by failing to comprehend subjectivity as a historical category.

Dialectically conceived "subjectivity" is historically formed and yet not reducible to historical determinations; historical subjectivity is reconstructed from the framework of reflective critique in that the limits of constitutive synthesis establish the range of possible experience. Only in such a reflective reconstruction of the genesis of subjectivity is it possible to distinguish between real possibilities and those modes of appearance that are but abstract illusions, e.g., existentialism's transcendence of historical domination. So conceived, the dialectical notion of subjectivity is a fundamental category of critical reason. In reflective reconstructions of self-formation processes, it is possible to show the pseudo-necessity of socially unnecessary motives and to thereby promote a reversal of consciousness that can dissolve the causality of these objective illusions.[9]

In *The Jargon of Authenticity* Adorno applies the method of immanent criticism to contemporary German existentialists (e.g., Buber, Jaspers, Heidegger, etc.). His basic thesis is that after World War II this philosophical perspective became an ideological mystification of human domination—while pretending to be a critique of alienation. Use of existentialistic terms became, Adorno argues, a jargon: a mode of magical expression which Walter Benjamin called an "aura." In the aura of existentialism the historical need for meaning and liberation was expressed, but in a way that mystified the actual relation between language and its objective content. Adorno's critique focuses on the jargon's incapacity to express the relation between language and truth, in that it breaks the dialectic of language by making the intended object appear present by the idealization inherent in the word itself. The jargon, therefore, falls into an objectivism that conceals the difference between philosophical reflection and the in-itselfness of the object of reflection. Such objectivism loses the intent of reflection to maintain a self-consciousness of the mediation of fact through the thinking subject. Consequently, in the jargon objective consciousness is compressed into self-experience, and an idealism results.

9. The methodological ideal of critical theory has been given a contemporary restatement in Jürgen Habermas, *Knowledge and Human Interests* (Boston, 1971), and *Theory and Practice* (Boston, 1973). The continuity of the tradition of critical theory has been argued by Trent Schroyer, *The Critique of Domination* (New York, 1973).

But the societal result of this idealistic tendency is that the jargon shares with modern advertising the ideological circularity of pretending to make present, in pure expressivity, an idealized form that is devoid of content; or, alternatively, just as the mass media can create a presence whose aura makes the spectator seem to experience a nonexistent actuality, so the jargon presents a gesture of autonomy without content. Adorno's analysis here continues Marx's analysis of the fetishism of commodities, in that the symbolisms of the jargon do not represent actual social relations but rather symbolize only the relations between abstract concepts. Lost in the fetishisms of the jargon is the actuality of the historical development of human consciousness. That the subject itself is formed, and deformed, by the objective configuration of institutions is forgotten, and thus reified, in the jargon's pathos of archaic primalness. Consequently, there is a loss of the objective context of human society and an idealistic compression of all historical consciousness into the sphere of self-experience. For example, Adorno cites Martin Buber's *I and Thou* and Paul Tillich's stress that religiosity is an end in itself, as instances of the shift to subjectivity as an in-it-selfness. In both cases the words are referred to the immediacy of life, to attitudinal and qualitative aspects of self-experience. One needs only to be a believer; the objective content of belief has been eclipsed in the subjectivization of objective content. To be a Christian seems to be a personal question—independent from the historical divinity of Christ. Without necessarily intending to do so, this extreme subjectivity transforms existentialistic language into a mystification of the objective constraints that block the autonomy and spontaneity of the historical subject.

Hegel proclaimed philosophy a "homecoming" that critically reconciled objective discord and subjective consciousness. His intent was to maintain a meaningful totality by the reflective mediations of critical reason. Reflection had as its aim the critique of abstractions, or in Marxian terms, of reifications. In this way Marx's work attempted to demonstrate the nonequivalence of exchange in the capitalist economy—thereby restoring to human consciousness a critical mediation of economic exploitation.

Adorno implies that contemporary German existentialism began from a higher level of capitalist development, in which the sociocultural antagonisms are much deeper than economic exploitation and extend into the subject's ego itself. Therefore, the haste with which the existentialists and their jargon attempt to achieve a reconciliation regardless of the objective processes of alienation which block meaning and autonomy, indicated only their awareness of the depth of the need. The resulting movement to a radical inwardness and its expressions of authenticity, freedom, etc., is an attempt to actualize these ideals outside of the objective social context: to fulfill heroic cultural models independent of the society. Behind these empty claims for freedom the socioeconomic processes of advanced capitalist integration continue, intensifying the dependence of all persons upon large organizational units for employment and welfare. The jargon's "blessings" conceal this objective context of unfreedom, and in the name of critical reflection the jargon joins hands with modern advertising in celebrating the meaningfulness of immediate experience.

Hence for Adorno, German existentialism and related genres, such as neoromantic lyric poetry (e.g., Rilke), come to a head in a mythic jargon that reduces the dialectical relationship of reflective critique to the objective content and context of subjectivity. The result is an ideology of the simple in which the primal sense of pure words is elevated in a futile attempt to overcome the "alienation" that remains linked to the political-economic framework of society.

Adorno's reconstruction of Heidegger's philosophy attempts to show that it becomes an ontology that retreats behind, rather than overcomes, the tradition of transcendental philosophy. In the universalization of transcendental subjectivity into Dasein, the empirical is totally lost and, as Adorno claims, an essence-mythology of Being emerges. This is exemplified in the claim that the primacy of Dasein is a realm beyond fact and essence and yet one which maintains itself as an identity. Whereas critical reason was able to show that maintenance of identity of consciousness presupposed a dialectic of subjective and objective reciprocity which was unified only in the constitutive activity of concrete subjectivity itself, Heidegger's notion of Dasein as both ontic and ontological stops the dialecticity of conscious existence in an idealistic elevation of the absolute subject. To quote Adorno:

> whatever praises itself for reaching behind the concepts of reflection—subject and object—in order to grasp something substantial, does nothing but reify the irresolvability of the concepts of reflection. It reifies the *impossibility* of reducing one into the other; into the in-itself (italics added).[10]

Adorno's thesis is that Heidegger's notion of selfness remains a reified tributary of Husserl's concept of

10. The mature statement of the notion of critical reason has been recently translated as *Negative Dialectik* (New York, 1973).

subject. This concept of subject, in attempting to overcome the pure possibility of the ontic, claims to be itself concrete. Hence, Heidegger dogmatically proclaims his concept of existence as something in opposition to identity—while at the same time he "continues the tradition of the doctrine of identity with his implicit definition of the self through its own preservation." Hence, Adorno examines the notions of "Dasein," "authenticity," "death," "care," etc., and shows that their use evades the issue of historical determinateness by means of a primary and absolute creative subject—which is, by definition, supposedly untouched by reification.

Hence, the aura of authenticity in Heidegger is that it names "nothing"; the "I" remains formal and yet pretends that the word contains content in-itself. For Adorno, Heidegger's existentialism is a new Platonism which implies that authenticity comes in the complete disposal of the person over himself—as if there were no determination emerging from the objectivity of history.

TRENT SCHROYER

Graduate Faculty of the
  New School for Social Research
February, 1973

AUTHOR'S NOTE

The author conceived the *Jargon of Authenticity* as part of the *Negative Dialectic*. However, he finally excluded that text from the latter work not only because its size grew disproportionate to the other parts, but also because the elements of linguistic physiognomy and sociology no longer fitted properly with the rest of the plan. The resistance against intellectual division of labor requires that this division of labor should be reflected on and not merely ignored. Certainly in intention and in theme the *Jargon* is philosophical. As long as philosophy was in line with its own nature, it also had content. However, in retreating to the ideal of its pure nature, philosophy cancels itself out. This thought was only developed in the book which was then still unfinished, while the *Jargon* proceeds according to this insight without, however, grounding it fully. Thus it was published earlier, as a kind of propaedeutic.

Insofar as the author has paid homage to the division of labor, he has at the same time all the more rudely challenged this division. He might be accused of philosophical, sociological, and aesthetic seduction without employing the traditional manner of keeping the categories separate—or maybe even of discussing them distinct from each other. Yet he would have to answer that a demand of this kind projects onto objects the desire for order which marks a classifying science, and which then proclaims that it is elevated by objects. The author, however, feels more inclined to give himself over to objects than to schematize like a schoolmaster—for the sake of an external standard: a standard which, questionably, has been brought to bear on the subject matter from the outside. This attitude determines itself by precisely the fact that the subject-matter elements of philosophy are intertwined. The common methodological ideal would break up this intimate unity. By means of such a unity of the subject matter, the unity of the author's own attempts should become all the more visible—for example, the unity of the author's philosophical essays with the essay, "Criticism of the Musician" from the *Dissonances*. What is aesthetically perceived in the bad form of language, and interpreted sociologically, is deduced from the untruth of the content which is posited with it: its implicit philosophy.

This makes for bad blood. Passages from Jaspers and idea blocks from Heidegger are treated on the same levels, and with that same linguistic attitude, which schoolmasters would probably reject with indignation. The text of the *Jargon*, however, contains enough evidence, from a truly inexhaustible wealth, to show that those men write in the same manner which they despise in their lesser followers as a justification of their own superiority. Their philosophemes show on what the jargon feeds, as well as its indirect suggestive force. The ambitious projects of German philosophy in the second half of the twenties concretized and articulated the direction into which the objective spirit of the time was drawn. This spirit remained what it was and thus speaks in the jargon even today. Only the criticism of these philosophical projects can objectively determine the mendacity which echoes in the vulgar jargon. The physiognomy of the vulgar jargon leads into what discloses itself in Heidegger.

It is nothing new to find that the sublime becomes the cover for something low. That is how potential victims are kept in line. But the ideology of the sublime no longer acknowledges itself without being disregarded. To show this fact might help to prevent criticism from stagnating in a vague and noncommittal suspicion of ideology, a suspicion which has itself fallen into ideology. Contemporary German ideology is careful not to pronounce definite doctrines, such as liberal or even elitist ones. Ideology has shifted into language. Social and anthropological changes have brought about this shift, though without breaking the veil. The fact that such language is actually ideology, i.e., societally necessary *Schein*, "appearance," can be shown from within it. This becomes obvious in the contradiction between its "how" and its "what." In its objective impossibility the jargon reacts toward the imminent impossibility of language. Language gives itself over either to the market, to balderdash, or to the predominating vulgarity. On the other hand language shoves its way toward the judge's bench, envelopes itself in judicial garb, and in that way asserts its privilege. The jargon is the happy synthesis which makes it explode.

Showing this has practical consequences. As irresistible as the jargon appears in present-day Germany, it is actually weak and sickly. The fact that the jargon has become an ideology unto itself destroys this ideology as soon as this fact is recognized. If the jargon were finally to become silent in Germany, part of that would have been accomplished for which skepticism, itself prejudiced, is praised—prematurely and without justification. The interested parties who use the jargon as a means of power, or depend on their public image for the jargon's social-psychological effect, will never wean themselves from it. There are others who will be embarrassed by the jargon. Even followers who believe in authority will shy away from ridiculousness, as soon as they feel the fragile nature of that authority to which they look for support. The jargon is the historically appropriate form of untruth in the Germany of the last years. For this reason one can discover a truth in the determinate negation of the jargon, a truth which refuses to be formulated in positive terms. Parts of the first sections were originally published in the third issue of the *Neue Rundschau* in 1963, and have been incorporated into the text.

June, 1967

THE Jargon
OF Authenticity

In the early twenties a number
of people active in philosophy, sociology, and theology,
planned a gathering. Most of them had shifted from
one creed to another. Their common ground was an
emphasis on a newly acquired religion, and not the
religion itself. All of them were unsatisfied with the
idealism which at that time still dominated the universities. Philosophy swayed them to choose, through freedom and autonomy, a positive theology such as had
already appeared in Kierkegaard. However, they were
less interested in the specific doctrine, the truth content of revelation, than in conviction. To his slight
annoyance, a friend, who was at that time attracted by
this circle, was not invited. He was—they intimated—
not authentic enough. For he hesitated before Kierkegaard's leap. He suspected that religion which is con-
jured up out of autonomous thinking would subordi-

nate itself to the latter, and would negate itself as the absolute which, after all, in terms of its own conceptual nature, it wants to be. Those united together were anti-intellectual intellectuals. They confirmed their mutual understanding on a higher level by excluding one who did not pronounce the same credo they repeated to one another. What they fought for on a spiritual and intellectual plane they marked down as their ethos, as if it elevated the inner rank of a person to follow the teaching of higher ideals; as if there were nothing written in the New Testament against the Pharisees. Even forty years later, a pensioned bishop walked out on the conference of a Protestant academy because a guest lecturer expressed doubt about the contemporary possibility of sacred music. He too had been warned against, and dispensed from, having dealings with people who do not toe the line; as though critical thought had no objective foundation but was a subjective deviation. People of his nature combine the tendency that Borchardt called a putting-themselves-in-the-right with the fear of reflecting their reflections —as if they didn't completely believe in themselves. Today, as then, they sense the danger of losing again what they call the concrete—of losing it to that abstraction of which they are suspicious, an abstraction which cannot be eradicated from concepts. They consider concretion to be promised in sacrifice, and first of all in intellectual sacrifice. Heretics baptized this circle "The Authentic Ones."

This was long before the publication of *Sein und Zeit.* Throughout this work Heidegger employed "authenticity," in the context of an existential ontology, as a specifically philosophical term. Thus in philosophy he molded that which the authentics strive for less theoretically; and in that way he won over to his side all those who had some vague reaction to that philosophy. Through him, denominational demands became dispensable. His book acquired its aura by describing the directions of the dark drives of the intelligentsia before 1933—directions which he described as full of insight, and which he revealed to be solidly coercive. Of course in Heidegger, as in all those who followed his language, a diminished theological resonance can be heard to this very day. The theological addictions of these years have seeped into the language, far beyond the circle of those who at that time set themselves up as the elite. Nevertheless, the sacred quality of the authentics' talk belongs to the cult of authenticity rather than to the Christian cult, even where—for temporary lack of any other available authority—its language resembles the Christian. Prior to any consideration of particular content, this language molds thought. As a consequence, that thought accommodates itself to the goal of subordination even where it aspires to resist that goal. The authority of the absolute is overthrown by absolutized authority. Fascism was not simply a conspiracy—although it was that—but it was something that came to life in the course of a powerful social development. Language provides it with a refuge. Within this refuge a smoldering evil expresses itself as though it were salvation.

In Germany a jargon of authenticity is spoken— even more so, written. Its language is a trademark of societalized chosenness, noble and homey at once—

sub-language as superior language. The jargon extends from philosophy and theology—not only of Protestant academies—to pedagogy, evening schools, and youth organizations, even to the elevated diction of the representatives of business and administration. While the jargon overflows with the pretense of deep human emotion, it is just as standardized as the world that it officially negates; the reason for this lies partly in its mass success, partly in the fact that it posits its message automatically, through its mere nature. Thus the jargon bars the message from the experience which is to ensoul it. The jargon has at its disposal a modest number of words which are received as promptly as signals. "Authenticity" itself is not the most prominent of them. It is more an illumination of the ether in which the jargon flourishes, and the way of thinking which latently feeds it. For a beginning, terms like "existential," "in the decision," "commission," "appeal," "encounter," "genuine dialogue," "statement," "concern," will do for examples. Not a few nonterminological terms of similar cast could be added to this list. Some, like "concern," a term still innocently used by Benjamin and verified in Grimm's dictionary, have only taken on such changed coloring since getting into this "field of tension"—a term that is also an appropriate example.

Thus the important thing is not the planning of an *Index Verborum Prohibitorum* of current noble nouns, but rather the examination of their linguistic function in the jargon. Certainly not all its words are noble nouns. At times it even picks up banal ones, holds them high and bronzes them in the fascist manner

6

which wisely mixes plebeian with elitist elements. Neoromantic poets who drank their fill of the precious, like George Hofmannsthal, by no means wrote their prose in the jargon. However, many of their intermediaries—like Gundolf—did so. The words become terms of the jargon only through the constellation that they negate, through each one's gesture of uniqueness. The magic that the singular word has lost is procured for it by manipulations—of whatever kind. The transcendence of the single word is a secondary one, one that is delivered ready from the factory, a transcendence which is a changeling said to be the lost original. Elements of empirical language are manipulated in their rigidity, as if they were elements of a true and revealed language. The empirical usability of the sacred ceremonial words makes both the speaker and listener believe in their corporeal presence. The ether is mechanically sprayed, and atomistic words are dressed up without having been changed. Thus they become more important than the jargon's so-called system. The jargon—objectively speaking, a system—uses disorganization as its principle of organization, the breakdown of language into words in themselves. Many of them, in another linguistic constellation, can be used without a glance at the jargon: "statement," where it is used in its fullest sense, in epistemology, to designate the sense of predicative judgments; "authentic" —already to be used with caution—even in an adjectival sense, where the essential is distinguished from the accidental; "inauthentic," where something broken is implied, an expression which is not immediately appropriate to what is expressed; "radio broadcasts of traditional music, music conceived in the categories of live performance, are grounded by the feeling of *as if,* of the inauthentic."[1] "Inauthentic" in that way becomes a "critical" term, in definite negation of something merely phenomenal. However, the jargon extracts authenticity, or its opposite, from every such transparent context. Of course one would never criticize a firm for using the word *Auftrag (commission),* when it has been assigned a commission. But possibilities of that sort remain narrow and abstract. Whoever overstrains them is paying tribute to a blank nominalistic theory of language, in which words are interchangeable counters, untouched by history.

Yet history does intrude on every word and withholds each word from the recovery of some alleged original meaning, that meaning which the jargon is always trying to track down. What is or is not the jargon is determined by whether the word is written in an intonation which places it transcendently in opposition to its own meaning; by whether the individual words are loaded at the expense of the sentence, its propositional force, and the thought content. In that sense the character of the jargon would be quite formal: it sees to it that what it wants is on the whole felt and accepted through its mere delivery, without regard to the content of the words used. It takes under its own control the preconceptual, mimetic element in language—for the sake of effect connotations. "Statement" thus wants to make believe that the existence of the speaker has communicated itself simultaneously

1. Theodor W. Adorno, *Der getreue Korrepitor* (Frankfurt, 1963) p. 218.

8

with his subject matter and has given the latter its dignity. The jargon makes it seem that without this surplus of the speaker the speech would already be inauthentic, that the pure attention of the expression to the subject matter would be a fall into sin. This formal element favors demagogic ends. Whoever is versed in the jargon does not have to say what he thinks, does not even have to think it properly. The jargon takes over this task and devaluates thought. That the whole man should speak is authentic, comes from the core. Thus something occurs which the jargon itself stylizes as "to occur." [2] Communication clicks and puts forth as truth what should instead be suspect by virtue of the prompt collective agreement. The tone of the jargon has something in it of the seriousness of the augurs, arbitrarily independent from their context or conceptual content, conspiring with whatever is sacred.

The fact that the words of the jargon sound as if they said something higher than what they mean suggests the term "aura." It is hardly an accident that Benjamin introduced the term at the same moment when, according to his own theory, what he understood by "aura" became impossible to experience. [3] As words that are sacred without sacred content, as frozen emanations, the terms of the jargon of authenticity

2. Later in the text Adorno refers to Heidegger's term *Ereignis*, which has been rendered as "event" in the standard translation of *Being and Time*. "To occur" our rendering of *sich ereignen*, has been chosen for lack of an English verb corresponding to the noun "event."

3. Cf. Walter Benjamin, *Schriften I* (Frankfurt, 1955), "Das Kunstwerk im Zeitalter seiner technischen Reproduzierbarkeit," p. 374. [English translation by Harry Zohn, in *Illuminations* (New York, 1968).]

are products of the disintegration of the aura. The latter pairs itself with an attitude of not being bound and thus becomes available in the midst of the de-mythified world; or, as it might be put in paramilitary modern German, it becomes *einsatzbereit,* mobilized. The perpetual charge against reification, a charge which the jargon represents, is itself reified. It falls under Richard Wagner's definition of a theatrical effect as the result of an action without agent, a definition which was directed against bad art. Those who have run out of holy spirit speak with mechanical tongues. The secret which is suggested, and from the beginning is not there, is a public one. First one can subtract the misused Dostoevski from the expressionist formula "each man is selected," which can be found in a play by Paul Kornfeld—who was murdered by the Nazis. Then the formula is good only for the ideological self-satisfaction of a lower middle class which is threatened and humbled by societal development. The jargon derives its own blessing, that of primalness, from the fact that it has developed as little in actuality as in spirit. Nietzsche did not live long enough to grow sick at his stomach over the jargon of authenticity: in the twentieth century he is the German resentment phenomenon par excellence. Nietzsche's "something stinks" would find its first justification in the strange bathing ceremony of the hale life:

> Sunday really begins on Saturday evening. When the tradesman straightens his shop, when the housewife has put the whole house into clean and shining condition, and has even swept the street in front of the house and freed it from all the dirt which it has collected dur-

ing the week; when, finally, even the children are bathed; then the adults wash off the week's dust, scrub themselves thoroughly; and go to the fresh clothes which are lying ready for them: when all of that is arranged, with rural lengthiness and care, then a deep warm feeling of resting settles down over the people.[4]

Expressions and situations, drawn from a no longer existent daily life, are forever being blown up as if they were empowered and guaranteed by some absolute which is kept silent out of reverence. While those who know better hesitate to appeal to revelation, they arrange, in their addiction to authority, for the ascension of the word beyond the realm of the actual, conditioned, and contestable; while these same people, even in private, express the word as though a blessing from above were directly composed into that word. That supreme state which has to be thought, but which also refuses being thought, is mutilated by the jargon. The latter acts as if it had possessed this state "from the beginning of time," as it might run in the jargon. What philosophy aims at, the peculiar character of philosophy which makes representation essential to it, causes all its words to say more than each single one. This characteristic is exploited by the jargon. The transcendence of truth beyond the meanings of individual words and propositional statements is attributed to the words by the jargon, as their immutable possession, whereas this "more" is formed only by the mediation of the constellation. According to its ideal, philosophical language goes beyond what it says by

4. Otto Friedrich Bollnow, *Neue Geborgenheit* (Stuttgart, 1956), p. 205.

means of what it says in the development of a train of thought. Philosophical language transcends dialectically in that the contradiction between truth and thought becomes self-conscious and thus overcomes itself. The jargon takes over this transcendence destructively and consigns it to its own chatter. Whatever more of meaning there is in the words than what they say has been secured for them once and for all as expression. The dialectic is broken off: the dialectic between word and thing as well as the dialectic, within language, between the individual words and their relations. Without judgment, without having been thought, the word is to leave its meaning behind. This is to institute the reality of the "more." It is to scoff, without reason, at that mystical language speculation which the jargon, proud of its simplicity, is careful not to remember. The jargon obliterates the difference between this "more" for which language gropes, and the in-itself of this more. Hypocrisy thus becomes an a priori, and everyday language is spoken here and now as if it were the sacred one. A profane language could only approach the sacred one by distancing itself from the sound of the holy, instead of by trying to imitate it. The jargon transgresses this rule blasphemously. When it dresses empirical words with aura, it exaggerates general concepts and ideas of philosophy —as for instance the concept of being—so grossly that their conceptual essence, the mediation through the thinking subject, disappears completely under the varnish. Then these terms lure us on as if they were the most concrete terms. Transcendence and concretion scintillate. Ambiguity is the medium of an attitude toward language which is damned by its favorite philosophy.[5]

But the untruth indicts itself by becoming bombastic. After a long separation a certain person wrote that he was existentially secure; it took some reflection to realize that he meant he had been sufficiently taken care of in regard to his finances. A center intended for international discussions—whatever they may be good for—is called the House of Encounters; the visible house, "firmly grounded in the earth," is turned into a sacred house through those gatherings—which are meant to be superior to discussions because they occur among existing and living individuals, although these individuals might just as well be engaged in discussion, for as long as they do not commit suicide they could hardly do anything other than exist. One's relation to his fellow man should be important prior to all content; for that purpose the jargon is satisfied with the shabby group-ethos of the youth movement, an indication that nothing is reaching either beyond the nose of the speaker, or beyond the capacity of the person who has only lately begun to be called his "partner." The jargon channels engagement into firm institutions and, furthermore, strengthens the most subaltern speakers in their self-esteem; they are already something because someone speaks from within them, even when that someone is nothing at all. The resonant directive

5. Cf. Martin Heidegger, *Sein und Zeit*, 3d ed. (Halle, 1931), pp. 217 ff. [English translation by John Macquarrie and Edward Robinson, *Being and Time* (New York, 1962). Subsequent page references from *Being and Time* will be to this translation.]

of the jargon, that its thought should not be too strenu-
ous, because otherwise it would offend the community,
also becomes for these people the guarantee of a higher
confirmation. This suppresses the fact that the language itself—through its generality and objectivity—
already negates the whole man, the particular speaking individual subject: the first price exacted by language is the essence of the individual. But through the
appearance that the whole man, and not thought,
speaks, the jargon pretends that, as a close-at-hand
manner of communication, it is invulnerable to de-
humanized mass communication—which is precisely
what recommends it to everyone's enthusiastic accept-
ance. Whoever stands behind his words, in the way in
which these words pretend, is safe from any suspicion
about what he is at that very moment about to do:
speak for others in order to palm something off on
them.

The word "statement" finally secures its alibi when
"true" is connected to it. By means of its prestige it
wants to endow the "for others" with the solidity of the
in-itself. For glorified man, who himself not too long
ago invented the term "death and glory squad," is
the ground of being for the jargon as well as the ad-
dressee of the statement; and it has become impossible
to distinguish between the two. The attribute "valid"
often sticks to "statement." The reason for this obviously lies in the fact that the emphatic experience,
which the word claims insistently, is no longer experienced by those who favor this word for the claim it
makes. A loudspeaker becomes necessary. "Statement"
wants to announce that something which was said has

come from the depth of the speaking subject; it is removed from the curse of surface communication. But at the same time communicative disorder disguises itself in the statement. Someone speaks and, thanks to the elevated term "statement," what he says is to be the sign of truth—as if men could not become caught up in untruth, as if they could not suffer martyrdom for plain nonsense. Prior to all content this shift indicts statement as soon as it wants to be such; it charges statement with being a lie. The listener is supposed to gain something from the statement because of its subjective reliability. This latter attribute, however, is borrowed from the world of wares. It is the claim of the consumer that even the spiritual should direct itself according to his will, against its own conceptual nature.

This admonition to the spirit silently dominates the whole climate of the jargon. The real and vain need for help is supposed to be satisfied by the pure spirit, merely by means of consolation and without action. The empty chatter about expression is the ideology complementary to that silencing which the status quo imposes on those who have no power over it, and whose claim is therefore hollow in advance. But whatever turns its back critically on the status quo has been discounted, by Germans in solid positions, as "without expressive value." Not least of all, statement is used as the club with which to assail the new art. That art's recalcitrance against traditional communicable sense has been reproached—as though from a higher viewpoint—by those whose aesthetic consciousness is not up to it. If one adds to a statement that it is "valid," then whatever at a given moment holds good, whatever is officially stamped, can be imputed to it as metaphysically authorized. The formula spares people the trouble of thinking about the metaphysics which it has dragged with it, or about the content of what has been stated.

The concept of statement appears in Heidegger as nothing less that the constituent of the *Da*, existence.[6] Behind this jargon is a determining doctrine of the I-thou relationship as the locale of truth—a doctrine that defames the objectivity of truth as thingly, and secretly warms up irrationalism. As such a relationship, communication turns into that transpsychological element which it can only be by virtue of the objectivity of what is communicated; in the end stupidity becomes the founder of metaphysics. Ever since Martin Buber split off Kierkegaard's view of the existential from Kierkegaard's Christology, and dressed it up as a universal posture, there has been a dominant inclination to conceive of metaphysical content as bound to the so-called relation of I and thou. This content is referred to the immediacy of life. Theology is tied to the determinations of immanence, which in turn want to claim a larger meaning, by means of their suggestion of theology: they are already virtually like the words of the jargon. In this process, nothing less is whisked away than the threshold between the natural and the supernatural. Lesser authentics raise their eyes reverently before death, but their spiritual attitude, infatuated with the living, disregards death. The thorn in theology, without which salvation is unthink-

6. *Ibid.*, p. 196.

able, is removed. According to the concept of theology, nothing natural has gone through death without metamorphosis. In the man-to-man relationship there can be no eternity now and here, and certainly not in the relationship of man to God, a relationship that seems to pat Him on the shoulder. Buber's style of existentialism draws its transcendence, in a reversed *analogia entis*, out of the fact that spontaneous relationships among persons cannot be reduced to objective poles. This existentialism remains the *Lebensphilosophie* out of which it came, in philosophical history, and which it abnegated: it overelevates the dynamism of mortality into the sphere of immortality.

Thus in the jargon transcendence is finally brought closer to men: it is the Wurlitzer organ of the spirit. The sermon in Huxley's *Brave New World* must have been written in the jargon. It was taped in order to be played when needed: to bring to reason the rebellious masses—by deep programmed emotion—in case they should once more band together. For advertising purposes the Wurlitzer organ humanizes the vibrato, once a carrier of subjective expression, by mechanically superimposing it on the mechanically produced sound. The jargon likewise supplies men with patterns for being human, patterns which have been driven out of them by unfree labor, if ever in fact traces of free labor did exist. Heidegger instituted authenticity against the they and against small talk, without deluding himself that there could be a complete leap between the two types of existentials that he deals with; for he knew that they merge into each other precisely because of their own dynamism. But he did not foresee that what he named authentic, once become word, would grow toward the same exchange-society anonymity against which *Sein und Zeit* rebelled. The jargon, which in Heidegger's phenomenology of small talk earned an honored position, marks the adept, in their own opinion, as untrivial and of higher sensibility; while at the same time that jargon calms the constantly festering suspicion of uprootedness.

In professional groups which, as they say, carry on intellectual work, but which are at the same time employed, dependent, or economically weak, the jargon is a professional illness. Among such groups a specific function is added to a general social one. Their culture and consciousness limp far behind that spirit which according to society's division of labor is their realm of activity. Through their jargon they aspire to remove this distance, to put themselves forward as sharers in higher culture (to them old hats still sound modern) as well as individuals with an essence of their own; the more innocent among them may quite frankly still call all that a *personal note*—using an expression from the era of handicrafts, from which the jargon in question has borrowed a lot. The stereotypes of the jargon support and reassure subjective movement. They seem to guarantee that one is not doing what in fact he is doing—bleating with the crowd—simply by virtue of his using those stereotypes to guarantee that one has achieved it all himself, as an unmistakably free person. The formal gesture of autonomy replaces the content of autonomy. Bombastically, it is called commitment, but it is heteronomously borrowed. That which pseudo-individualizing attends to in the culture industry, the jargon attends to among those who have contempt for the culture industry. This is the German symptom of progressive half-culture. It seems to be invented for those who feel that they have been judged by history, or at least that they are falling, but who still strut in front of their peers as if they were an interior elite.

The importance of this jargon is not to be underestimated simply because a small group writes it. Innumerable real-life people speak it, from the student who in his exam lets himself go on about authentic encounter, to the bishop's press secretary who asks: Do you believe that God addresses only our reason? Their unmediated language they receive from a distributor. In the theological conversations of Dr. Faustus' students, in Auerbach's den of 1945, Thomas Mann intuited with precise irony most of the habits of modern German—though he no longer had much occasion to observe them. There certainly were appropriate models before 1933, but only after the war, when National Socialist language became unwanted, did the jargon gain omnipresence. Since then the most intimate interchange has taken place between the written and the spoken word. Thus one will be able to read printed jargon which unmistakably imitates radio voices that have themselves drawn on written works of authenticity. Mediated and immediate elements are mediated through each other in frightful ways. And since they are synthetically prepared, that which is mediated has become the caricature of what is natural. The jargon no longer knows primary and secondary communities, and by the same token it knows no parties. This development has a real basis. The institutional and psychological superstructure, which in 1930 Kracauer diagnosed as a culture of employees, deluded the celluloid-collar proletariat, who were then threatened by the immediacy of losing their jobs. It deluded them into believing that they were something special. Through this delusion the superstructure made them toe the bourgeois line, while in the meantime, thanks to a lasting market boom, that superstructure has become the universal ideology of a society which mistakes itself for a unified middle class. They let themselves be confirmed in this attitude by a uniform mode of speech, which eagerly welcomes the jargon for purposes of collective narcissism. This applies not only to those who speak it but also to the objective spirit. The jargon affirms the reliability of the universal by means of the distinction of having a bourgeois origin, a distinction which is itself authorized by the universal. Its tone of approved selectivity seems to come from the person himself. The greater advantage in all this is that of good references. It makes no difference what the voice that resonates in this way says; it is signing a social contract. Awe, in face of that existent which pretends to be more than it is, beats down all that is unruly. One is given to understand that that which occurs is so deep that language could not unhallow what has been said by saying it. Pure clean hands recoil from the thought of changing anything in the valid property-and-authority relationships; the very sound of it all makes that idea contemptible, as the merely ontic is to Heidegger. One can trust anyone who babbles this jargon; people wear it in their buttonholes, in place of the currently disreputable party badge. The pure tone drips with positivity, without needing to stoop too far—pleading for what is all too compromised; one escapes even the long-since-socialized suspicion of ideology. In the jargon that division between the destructive and the constructive, with which fascism had cut off critical thought, comfortably hibernates. Simply to be there becomes the merit of a thing. It is guaranteed in the protection of the double sense of the positive: as something existent, given, and as something worthy of being affirmed. Positive and negative are reified prior to living experience, as though they were valid prior to all living experience of them; as though it was not thought that first of all determined what is positive or negative; and as though the course of such determination were not itself the course of negation.

The jargon secularizes the German readiness to view men's positive relation to religion as something immediately positive, even when the religion has disintegrated and been exposed as something untrue. The undiminished irrationality of rational society encourages people to elevate religion into an end in itself, without regard to its content: to view religion as a mere attitude, as a quality of subjectivity. All this at the cost of religion itself. One needs only to be a believer—no matter what he believes in. Such irrationality has the same function as putty. The jargon of authenticity inherits it, in the childish manner of Latin primers which praise the love of the fatherland in-itself—which praise the *viri patriae amantes*, even when the fatherland in question covers up the most atrocious deeds. Sonnemann has described this phenomenon as not being able to get rid of a benevolent attitude which at all costs defends order, even an order in which all these things are not in order. What things? According to the logic of the sentence they ought only to be accidentals, but instead they are strikingly essential: "poisonous exhaust emissions, pressing taboos, insincerity, resentments, hidden hysteria on all sides." What remains then of the orderliness of the order? Obviously, it needs first to be created.[7] Benevolence is identical with being predecided. What is affirmative and wholesome doubles the curse of evil. Through marriage offers, the jargon guides the *petit bourgeois* to a positive attitude toward life. It fastidiously prolongs the innumerable events which are to make attractive to men a life by which they otherwise would be disgusted—and which they would soon come to consider unbearable. That religion has shifted into the subject, has become religiosity, follows the trend of history. Dead cells of religiosity in the midst of the secular, however, become poisonous. The ancient force, which according to Nietzsche's insight nourishes everything, should enter completely into the profane; instead it preserves itself in an unreflected manner and elevates limitation, which abhors reflection, to the level of virtue.

All experts in the jargon, from Jaspers on down, unite in praise of positivity. Only the careful Heidegger avoids a too open-hearted affirmation for its own sake, and indirectly pays his dues. He is eager and genuine about it. But Jaspers writes, unashamedly: "Actually

7. Ulrich Sonnemann, *Das Land der unbegrenzten Zumutbarkeiten* (Reinbek bei Hamburg, 1963), pp. 196 ff.

only that man can remain in the world who lives out from something which in every case he possesses only through commitment." [8] To which he adds: "Only the person who commits himself freely is proof against a disillusioned revolt against himself." [9] It is true that his philosophy of existence has chosen, as its patron saint, Max Weber, who stood up proudly without illusions. Nevertheless, he is interested in religion, no matter of what kind. He is interested in it provided it is ready at hand, because it guarantees the required commitment; or simply because it exists, whether or not it fits with the notion of independent philosophy, which Jaspers reserves for himself as if it were a personal privilege:

> Whoever is true to transcendence in the form of such a belief should never be attacked, so long as he does not become intolerant. For in the believing person only destruction can take place; he can perhaps remain open to philosophizing, and risk the corresponding burden of a doubting, which is inseparable from human existence; yet he has the positivity of an historical existence as his reference and measure, which bring him irreplaceably back to himself. About these possibilities we do not speak.[10]

When autonomous thought still had confidence in its humane realization, it behaved less humanely. In

8. Karl Jaspers, *Die geistige Situation der Zeit*, 5th ed. (Berlin, 1947), pp. 169 ff. [English translation by Eden and Cedar Paul, *Man in the Modern Age* (New York, 1957). All quotations from this work are translated from the original German.]

9. *Ibid.*

10. *Ibid.*, pp. 127 ff.

the meantime, the less philosophers are infected with philosophy the more innocently do they let the cat out of the bag; a bag which prominent ones weave like Norns. Sentences from O. F. Bollnow sound like this:

> Therefore it seems especially meaningful that in poetry, above all in the lyric of the last years, after all the experiences of dread, a new feeling, of affirmation of being, is beginning to make its appearance, a joyful and thankful harmony with the very existence of man, as it is; a harmony with the world as it confronts man. Two of these poets in particular should receive special attention here: Rilke and Bergengruen. Bergengruen's last volume of poetry *Die Heile Welt* (Munich, 1950), p. 272, closes with the confession: "What came from pain was only transient. And my ear heard nothing but songs of praise." In other words, it is a feeling of thankful agreement with existence. And Bergengruen certainly is not a poet who could be criticized for a cheap optimism. In this feeling of deep thankfulness he comes close to Rilke, who also, at the close of his way, is able to state: "Everything breathes and returns thanks. Oh you troubles of the night, how you sank without a trace." [11]

Bergengruen's volume is only a few years closer to us than the time when Jews who had not been completely killed by the gas were thrown living into the fire, where they regained consciousness and screamed. The poet, who can certainly not be criticized for cheap optimism, and the philosophically minded pedagogue who evaluates him, heard nothing but songs of praise. In a preliminary definition we call this inner state of man an attitude of trustful reliance. Thus the task is set: to

11. Bollnow, *Geborgenheit*, pp. 26 ff.

examine the nature of this state of the soul in order to find its possibilities.[12] Bollnow found the best of all possible names for this task, which in the face of horror can no longer even appease us by virtue of its ridiculousness—he called it *Seinsgläubigkeit,* faith unto Being.[13] The fact that the term reminds us of *Deutschgläubigkeit,* faith unto German nationality, is certainly accidental. Once faith unto Being is achieved, there is no stopping before we reach a "positive relation to the world and life" [14] and "constructive work toward the overcoming of existentialism." [15] What remains after the removal of existential bombast are religious customs cut off from their religious content. There is no recognition of the fact that cult forms, the subject matter of folklore, like empty shells, outlive their mystery. This state of affairs is in fact defended with the aid of the jargon. All of this is an insult not only to thought but also to religion, which was once man's promise of eternal bliss, while now authenticity contents itself resignedly with an "ultimately hale world." [16] "In the following we can distinguish these two forms— for the sake of a convenient terminology—as hope which has a determined content and hope which has an undetermined content; or, briefly, as relative and absolute hope." [17] This pitiful concept-splitting applies itself to the question of "existence welfare." It makes no difference to a follower to what he attaches him-

12. *Ibid.,* p. 51.
13. *Ibid.,* p. 57.
14. *Ibid.,* p. 61.
15. *Ibid.*
16. *Ibid.,* p. 63.
17. *Ibid.,* p. 100.

25

self at a given moment. He praises this as his capacity for enthusiasm. Whether such a man ranks himself as lowbrow, middlebrow, or highbrow, he can consider that "hale" refers to the haleness of the soul, or right living, or social enclaves not yet taken over by industrialism, or simply places where Nietzsche and the Enlightenment have not yet been heard of; or chaste conditions in which girls hold their maidenhood intact until they get married. We should not oppose to the catch-word of "shelteredness," the equally worn-out idea of the dangerous life; who wouldn't want to live without anxiety in this world of terrors? But shelteredness, as an existential value, turns from something longed for and denied into a presence which is now and here, and which is independent of what prevents it from being. It leaves its trace in the violation of the word: the reminiscence of what is hedged-in and safely bordered remains joined to that element of short-sighted particularity which out of itself renews the evil against which no one is sheltered. Home will only come to be when it has freed itself from such particularity, when home has negated itself as universal. The feeling of shelteredness makes itself at home with itself, and offers a holiday resort in place of life. A landscape becomes uglier when an admirer disrupts it with the words "how beautiful." The same happens to customs, habits, institutions which barter themselves away by stressing their own naïveté instead of by changing it. All talk of shelteredness is indicted by Kogon's report that the worst atrocities in the concentration camps were committed by the younger sons of farmers. The

26

general situation in the country, which is the model for the feeling of shelteredness, pushes disinherited sons into barbarousness. The logic of the jargon constantly smuggles in what is limited, finally even situations of material want, under the guise of positivity; and presses for their being eternally instituted at just that moment when, thanks to the state of human achievements, such a limitation no longer needs in reality to exist. A spirit which makes this limitation its cause hires itself out as the lackey of what is evil.

In the higher ranks of the hierarchy of authenticity, however, negativities are also served. Heidegger even requisitions the concept of destruction which is tabooed in the lower ranks, together with the blackness of fear, sorrow, and death. Jaspers occasionally blares out the opposite of Bollnow's *Geborgenheit*, shelteredness: "Today philosophy is the only possibility for one who is consciously unsheltered." [18] But the positive, like a tumbler doll, cannot be kept down. Danger, hazard, risking one's life, and the whole characteristic shudder, are not taken all that seriously. One of the Ur-authentic ones in her time remarked that in the innermost core of Dostoyevsky's hell the light of salvation shone again. She had to swallow the reply that hell was then an awfully short railroad tunnel. Some prominent authentic ones—a little reluctantly—put it like the parish preacher; they say they would rather harvest on burned earth. They are no less clever than social psychology, which has observed that negative judgments, of no

18. Jaspers, *Die geistige Situation,* p. 128.

matter what content, give a better chance of being affirmed than do positive judgments.[19] Nihilism turns into farce, into mere method, as has already happened to Cartesian doubt. The question—a favorite prerequisite of the jargon—must sound all the more radical the more loyally it directs itself to the kind of answer which can be everything except radical. Here is an elementary example from Jaspers:

> Existential philosophy would be lost immediately, if it once again believed that it knows what man is. It would again give us sketches of how to investigate human and animal life in its typical forms; it would again become anthropology, psychology, sociology. Its meaning is only possible when it remains groundless in its concreteness. It awakens what it does not know; it lightens and moves, but it does not fix and hold. For the man who is underway, this philosophy is the expression through which he maintains himself in his direction; the means toward preserving his highest moments—so that he can make them real through his life. . . . Insight into existence, because it remains without an object, leads to no conclusion.[20]

Exactly. A concerned tone is ominously struck up: no answer would be serious enough; every answer, no matter of what content, would be dismissed as a limiting concretization. But the effect of this remorseless intransigence is friendly; the man never pins himself

19. Cf. Gruppenexperiment, *Frankfurter Beiträge zur Soziologie* (Frankfurt, 1955), II, 482 ff.
20. Jaspers, *Die geistige Situation,* pp. 146–47.

down: the world is all too dynamic. The old Protestant theme of absurd belief, grounding itself in the subject, converted itself from Lessing to Kierkegaard into the pathos of existence. This pathos existed in opposition to its result, the reified world seen as coagulated and alien to the subject. That old theme allies itself strategically with the critique of positive science—science from which, as Kierkegaard's thesis ran, the subject has disappeared. At the cost of any possible answer, the radical question becomes what is substantial unto itself. Risk without hazard. Know-how and range of income are the only factors which determine whether one appears on the scene sheltered or has to start out without security. Even those who are not sheltered are safe as long as they join the chorus. This is what makes possible passages like the one from Heinz Schwitzke's *Three Fundamental Theses for Television:*

> This is totally different in the sermon. Here a clerical speaker professed his credo for more than ten minutes, out of his own depths, in the existential manner; a single, never-changing close-up. Thanks to the noble humane power of conviction that radiated out from him, not only did his words, which were testified to by his pictorial presence, become completely credible, but the listener totally forgot the mediating apparatus. In front of the television screen, as if in the house of God, there formed itself a sort of parish among the accidental viewers, who felt as if they were being confronted with the immediate presence of the speaker, and through him felt committed to the subject matter of his sermon, God's word. There is no other explanation for this surprising occurrence than the supreme importance of the speaking person, the person who has enough courage and ethos to place himself in the breach, and to serve

nothing but the subject matter which he stands for and the listeners to whom he knows he can relate.[21]

This is authenticity's funky commercial. The "word" of the preacher, as if his and God's were one without question, is testified to not by his "pictorial presence," but at best by behavior whose trustworthiness supports the credibility of his statements.

If, thanks to the appearance of the preacher, one forgets the mediating equipment, then the jargon of authenticity, which takes pleasure in this situation, is committing itself to the philosophy of As If: through stage-setting, the now and here of a cult action is simulated, an action which through its omnipresence is annulled on television. But, by the existential manner in which the preacher makes public profession of himself, from out of himself, "in a never changing close-up," we need only to understand the self-evident fact that the preacher, who after all had no other choice, was projected as an empirical person onto the screen and in this way, perhaps, had a sympathetic effect on many people. That he formed a community cannot be proven. The notion that he had to throw himself into the breach, with his whole substance and existence, is imported from the sphere of risk. Still, for that preacher who details on television why the church is too narrow for him there is no risk at all: neither of contradiction from outside nor of inner necessity. If in fact, hemmed in between microphone and floodlight, he had to suffer through moments of temp-

21. Heinz Schwitzke, "Drei Grundthesen zum Fernsehen," in *Rundfunk und Fernsehen*, II (1953), 11 ff.

tation, the jargon would have been right there waiting with additional praise for his existentiality. The benefit of the negative is transferred to the positive, as though by a single stroke of the pen: positive negativeness to warm the heart. These dark words are numinous, just like Bollnow's whitewashed Sunday words—as close to rejoicing as the dreadful trumpet has always been. Just as the jargon uses the double sense of the word "positive," it uses the ambiguity of the term "metaphysics," according to whether at a given moment one prefers nothingness or being. On the one hand metaphysics means involvement with metaphysical themes, even if the metaphysical content is contested; on the other hand it means the affirmative doctrine of the transcendent world, in the Platonic model. In this shifting metaphysical need, that state of the spirit which long ago made itself known in Novalis' *On Christendom or Europe*, or which the young Lukács called transcendental homelessness, has come down to culturally defined knowledge. The theological freeing of the numinous from ossified dogma has, ever since Kierkegaard, involuntarily come to mean its partial secularization. In mystical heresy, the unsatisfiable purification of the divine from myth, which loves to tremble in the gesture of deeply involved questioning, hands the divine over to whoever relates to it in any way. Liberal theology is suddenly reborn, since content is to be found only in a relation, the other pole of which removes itself from all definition as the "absolutely indifferent," and marks all definition with the blemish of reification. Complete demythologization totally reduces transcendence to an abstraction, to a concept. Enlightenment, which the *viri obscuri*[22] accuse, triumphs in their thought. In the same movement of the spirit, however, the positing power of the subject, veiled unto itself, again conjures up the myth inherent in all dialectical theology. That subjective power's highest value, as absolutely different, is blind. Under compulsion the *viri obscuri* praise commitments instead of jumping into speculation which alone could justify their own commitments to their radical questioners. Their relationship to speculation is confused. One needs it because one wants to be deep, yet one shies away from it because of its intellectual nature. One would prefer to reserve it for the gurus. The others still confess their groundlessness, in order to give character to the paths of offered salvation, which are reputed to be successful in extreme even if imaginary danger. However, they find nothing but groundless thinking as soon as thinking refuses, through its attitude, to support from the outset those commitments which are as unavoidable in authenticity as is the happy ending in movies. If the happy ending is lacking, then among the existential authentics existentialism itself has nothing to laugh at.

> Only against this background does the whole greatness of the existential ethic reveal itself. It once again actualizes, on the ground of modern historical relativism, a decidedly moral stance. But in precisely that sense a danger is given; that danger which comes to expression in the possibility of an existential adven-

22. [*Viri obscuri:* obscurantists, enemies of enlightenment. Historical reference to fictive humanist (fifteenth and sixteenth century) authors of letters against late forms of Scholasticism.]

turism. Having become fully unconditioned in regard to content, and without any of that constancy which resides in fidelity, the adventurer enjoys the risk of his engagement as a last and most sublime pleasure. Precisely in the unconditioned state of any given momentary engagement, the existentialist is especially exposed to the temptation of inconstancy and of faithlessness.[23]

All of these words draw from language, from which they are stolen, the aroma of the bodily, unmetaphorical; but in the jargon they become quietly spiritualized. In that way they avoid the dangers of which they are constantly palavering. The more earnestly the jargon sanctifies its everyday world, as though in a mockery of Kierkegaard's insistence on the unity of the sublime and the pedestrian, the more sadly does the jargon mix up the literal with the figurative:

Heidegger's final remark aims at this fundamental meaning of residing for all human existence, and in this remark he focuses on the "need for residences" as one of the great difficulties of our time: "The true need for residence," he says here, "consists not first of all in the absence of residences," although this need should by no means be taken lightly; but behind this need a deeper one is hidden, that man has lost his own nature and so cannot come to rest. "The true need for residence consists in the fact that mortals must first learn to reside." But to learn to reside means: to grasp this necessity, that, in the face of what is threatening, man should make for himself a sheltering space and should settle into it with a trustful reliance. But, then, inversely, the possibility of this settling down is again connected in a menacing way with the availability of residences.[24]

23. Bollnow, *Geborgenheit,* pp. 37 f.
24. *Ibid.,* p. 170.

The Being of the sheltering space of shelteredness is simply derived from the necessity that man should "make for himself" such a space. The linguistic carelessness, in the unresisting mechanism of the jargon, admittedly lays shelteredness bare, as if out of compulsion; lays it bare as something that is merely posited. However, that which announces itself, in the game about the need for residences, is more serious than the pose of existential seriousness. It is the fear of unemployment, lurking in all citizens of countries of high capitalism. This is a fear which is administratively fought off, and therefore nailed to the platonic firmament of stars, a fear that remains even in the glorious times of full employment. Everyone knows that he could become expendable as technology develops, as long as production is only carried on for production's sake; so everyone senses that his job is a disguised unemployment. It is a support that has arbitrarily and revocably pinched off something from the total societal product, for the purpose of maintaining the status quo.[25] He who has not been given a life ticket could in principle be sent away tomorrow. That migration of people could continue which the dictators already once before set in motion and channeled into Auschwitz. Angst, busily distinguished from innerworldly, empirical fear, need by no means be an existential value. Since it is historical, it appears in fact that those who are yoked into a society which is societalized, but contradictory to the deepest core, con-

25. Cf. Theodor W. Adorno, *Eingriffe: Neun kritische Modelle* (Frankfurt, 1963), p. 137.

stantly feel threatened by what sustains them. They feel threatened without ever being able in specific instances to concretize this threat from the whole of society. But in shelteredness the declassed person has his clumsy triumph—the declassed man who knows what he can get away with. On the one hand he has nothing to lose; on the other hand, the overadministrated world of today still respects the compromise structure of bourgeois society, to the extent that that society—in its own interest—stops short before the ultimate, the liquidation of its members, stops short because, in the massive plans of its industry, it has the means of delay at its disposal. So Jaspers' "existence welfare" and social welfare—administrated grace—come into contact. On the social ground of the jargon's reinterpretation of complete negativity into what is positive, we suspect the coercive self-confidence of the uneasy consciousness. Even our cheap suffering from the loss of meaning, a suffering long since automatized into a formula, is not simply that emptiness which has grown up through the whole movement of the Enlightenment—as the more demanding *viri obscuri* willingly describe it. There are reports of *taedium vitae* even during periods of unchallenged state religion; it was as common among the Fathers of the Church as among those who carry over into the jargon Nietzsche's judgment about modern nihilism, and who imagine that in that way they have gone beyond both Nietzsche and nihilism—Nietzsche's concept of which they have simply turned upside down. Socially, the feeling of meaninglessness is a reaction to the wide-reaching freeing from work which takes place under conditions of continuing social unfreedom. The free time of the subjects withholds from them the freedom which they secretly hope for; their free time chains them to the ever-same, the apparatus of production—even when this apparatus is giving them a vacation. With this situation they are forced to compare the obvious possibilities, and they grow the more confused the less the closed façade of consciousness, which is modeled after that of society, lets through the conception of a possible freedom.

At the same time, in the feeling of meaninglessness which is the high-bourgeois expression of real need, the permanent threat of destruction is assimilated by consciousness. What this consciousness dreads it turns in such a way that the threat seems to be an innate part of it, and thus it weakens that element of the threat which can no longer be grasped in human terms. The fact that on all sides meaning of every kind seems to be impotent against evil, that the latter yields no meaning at all, and that the assertion of meaning may even promote evil, is registered as a lack of metaphysical content, especially in regard to religious and social commitments. The falseness of this reinterpretation, using a mode of cultural criticism with which the stingy pathos of the authentics joins in, regularly becomes visible in a particular fact: the fact that past ages—whichever one prefers—ranging from Biedermeier to Pelasgic, appear as the ages of immanent meaning. Such reinterpretation follows an inclination to set back the clock politically and socially, to bring to an end the dynamism inherent in a society which still, through the administrative measures of the most powerful cliques, appears to be all too open. As its present form can expect nothing good from such a dynamic, it stubbornly blinds itself to the recognition that the cure which society offers is itself the evil that it fears. This is brought to a head in Heidegger. Cleverly, he couples the appeal of unromantic, incorruptible purity with the prophecy of a saving element which, in consequence, can present itself as nothing other than this purity itself. The hero of *Mahagonny* joined the wailing about a world in which there is nothing to hold on to. In Heidegger, as well as in the Brecht of the didactic plays, this is followed by the proclamation of compulsory order as salvation. The lack of something to hold on to is the mirror reflection of its opposite, of unfreedom. Only because mankind failed to define itself did it grope for determination through something else: something that was safely out of the reach of the dialectical movement. The anthropological condition of so-called human emptiness, which for the sake of contrast the authentics are accustomed to daub out as an unhappy, but inevitable, consequence of the demystified world, could be changed. The longing for some completing factor could be fulfilled, as soon as it was no longer denied—but not fulfilled, of course, through the injection of a spiritual meaning or a merely verbal substitution. The social constitution essentially trains mankind for the reproduction of itself, and the compulsion extends itself into society's psychology, as soon as it loses its external power. Thanks to the factor of self-preservation, which has blown itself up into a totality, the following happens: what man is anyway once more becomes his goal. Perhaps with this nonsense the appearance of meaninglessness might also disappear, the eagerly assured nothingness of the subject, a shadow of the state in which each person is literally his own neighbor. If it is the case that no metaphysical thought was ever created which has not been a constellation of elements of experience, then, in the present instance, the seminal experiences of metaphysics are simply diminished by a habit of thought which sublimates them into metaphysical pain and splits them off from the real pain which gave rise to them. The jargon's whole hatred is directed against this consciousness. No distinction is made between Marx and the superstition of race:

> Marxism, psychoanalysis, and racial theory are today the most widespread deceptions of mankind. The directly brutal in hatred and praise, as it has come to dominance in human existence, finds its expression in these systems of thought; in Marxism, in the manner in which the mass postulates community; in psychoanalysis, in the way it seeks mere existence satisfaction; in racial theory, in the way it wants to be better than the other. . . . Without sociology no political strategy can be carried out. Without psychology no one becomes master of the reigning confusion, in his converse with himself and with the others. Without anthropology we would lose our consciousness of the dark causes of that in which we possess ourselves. . . . No sociology can tell what fate I want, no psychology can clarify what I am, authentic being of man cannot be bred as race. Everywhere is the boundary of that which can be planned and made. For Marxism, psychoanalysis, and theory of race have characteristically destructive attributes. As Marxism thinks that it uncovers all spiritual being as Superstructure, psychoanalysis does the same in exposing spiritual being as sublimation of repressed drives. What, then, is still called culture is structured

like an obsessive neurosis. Theory of race causes a conception of history which is without hope. Negative selection of the best will soon bring about the ruin of authentic humanity; or, it is the nature of man to produce during this process the highest possibilities in a mixture of races, in order to leave behind ad infinitum the marrowless average existence of his remains, after the mixing has come to an end in the course of a few centuries. All three tendencies are apt to destroy what has seemed to be of value for men. They are especially the ruin of anything absolute, for, as knowledge, they make themselves a false absolute which recognizes everything else as conditioned. Not only has God to fall but also every form of philosophical belief. Both the highest and the lowest are labeled with the same terminology and, judged, step into nothingness.[26]

The practical usability of the enlightening disciplines is condescendingly granted in the beginning only to prevent more effectively any reflection on the truth content of criticism: by arousing our indignation at the desire to destroy. Passionate grief about obliviousness to being is given the appearance of the essential—to the point where one would rather like to forget all Being. All of that is more ominously attended to in *Der Grüne Heinrich*:

There is an old saying which maintains that one must not only tear down but must also know how to build up; a commonplace constantly employed by cheery and superficial people who are uncomfortably confronted with an activity which demands a decision from them. This way of speaking is in place where something is superficially settled or is denied out of stupid inclination; otherwise, though, it is unintelligible. For one is

26. Jaspers, *Die geistige Situation*, pp. 142 ff.

not always tearing down, in order to build again; on the contrary, one tears things down eagerly in order to win free space for light and air, which appear as it were by themselves, wherever some obstructing object is removed. When one looks matters right in the face and treats them in an upright manner, then nothing is negative, but all is positive—to use this old saw.[27]

Then the old warriors had an easier time of it: they had no need of old saws; they only needed to breathe sense into doubters with the cudgel of fate and Nordic manhood. But they already had the jargon at their disposal:

An extreme intensification of all activity, and a sharpening of all creative powers, even the great political event as such, mark our time; and to the eyes of philosophy they have physically presented this phenomenon in its authenticity and unvarnished originality. Philosophy has grasped this phenomenon as a condition of the highest philosophical relevance, in order to let itself be led, through its content and problematic structure, to a full and pure understanding of man and the world. . . . Human existence is not meaningless: that is the categorical assertion with which this existence itself confronts the philosophy of life, in order to assert itself in opposition to and over against that philosophy. . . . To say yes to fate and to negate it in spite of that, to suffer it and yet to dominate it, i.e., to face it and to take one's stand against it, that is the attitude of true humanity. This attitude corresponds to the ideal image of man because it represents nothing

27. Gottfried Keller, *Der Grüne Heinrich*, IV, 2, quoted in Friedrich Pollock, "Sombarts Widerlegung des Marxismus," in *Beihefte zum Archiv für die Geschichte des Sozialismus und der Arbeiterbewegung*, ed. Carl Grünberg (Leipzig, 1926), III, 63.

but the essence of man, universally valid and removed from all ties to time. At the same time, and at one with it, this attitude defines the deep and genuine meaning of fate, that meaning which has nothing to do with fatalism, a meaning to which especially a German opens himself. For the man of Nordic blood, this meaning takes on a deeply religious content and grounds what for him means his bond with fate and his belief in fate.[28]

Language uses the word "meaning" for the harmless epistemological intentional object of Husserl, as well as for the purpose of saying that something is justified as meaningful; as one would speak, for instance, of the meaning of history. It remains true that the factual particular has meaning to the extent that the whole, above all the system of society, appears in it; that the dispersed facts are always more than what they immediately seem, even if such meaning is madness. The search for meaning as that which something is authentically, and as that which is hidden in it, pushes away, often unnoticed and therefore all the faster, the question as to the right of this something. Analysis of meaning becomes the norm in this demand, not only for the signs but also for that which they refer to. The sign system of language, by its mere existence, takes everything, to begin with, into something that is held in readiness by society; and it defends this society in its own form prior to all content. This is what reflection stands firm against. However, the jargon drifts with the current, and would be glad

28. From Wilhelm Grebe, *Der deutsche Mensch: Untersuchungen zur Philosophie des Handelns* (Berlin, 1937).

to increase it, in union with the regressive formations of consciousness.

In its semantic directions positivism has constantly noted the historical break between language and that which it expresses. Linguistic forms, as reified—and only through reification do they become forms—have outlived what they once referred to, together with the context of that reference. The completely demythologized fact would withhold itself from language; through the mere act of intending the fact becomes an other—at least measured in terms of its idol of pure accessibility. That without language there is no fact remains, even so, the thorn in the flesh and the theme of positivism, since it is here that the stubbornly mythical remainder of language is revealed. Mathematics is, for good reason, the primal model of positivistic thought—even in its function as a languageless system of signs. Looked at in reverse, the tenacious residuum of what is archaic in language becomes fruitful only where language rubs itself critically against it; the same archaic turns into a fatal mirage when language spontaneously confirms and strengthens it. The jargon shares with positivism a crude conception of the archaic in language; neither of them bothers about the dialectical moment in which language, as if it were something else, wins itself away from its magical origins, language being entangled in a progressing demythologization. That particular neglect authorizes the social using of linguistic anachronism. The jargon simply ennobles the antiquity of language, which the positivists just as simply long to eradicate—along with all expression in language. The disproportion between language and the rationalized society drives the authentics to plunder language, rather than to drive it on, through greater sharpness, to its proper due. They don't fail to notice that one cannot speak absolutely without speaking archaically; but what the positivists bewail as retrogressive the authentics eternalize as a blessing.

For them that block which language piles up before the expression of undiminished experience becomes an altar. If it does not allow itself to be broken through, then it offers us simply the omnipotence and indissolubility of what was precipitated into language. But the archaic takes vengeance on the jargon, whose greed for the archaic violates the proper distance. The archaic is objectified for a second time. In its example is repeated that which in any case happened to language historically. The nimbus in which the words are being wrapped, like oranges in tissue paper, takes under its own direction the mythology of language, as if the radiant force of the words could not yet quite be trusted. Mixed with artificial coloring the words themselves, released from the relation to what is thought, are to speak a relation which should change them and so always demythologizes them. Language mythology and reification become mixed with that element which identifies language as antimythological and rational. The jargon becomes practicable along the whole scale, reaching from sermon to advertisement. In the medium of the concept the jargon becomes surprisingly similar to the habitual practices of advertising. The words of the jargon and those like *Jägermeister, Alte Kloster-frau, Schänke,*[29] are all of a piece. They exploit the happiness promised by that which had to pass on to the shadows. Blood is drawn from that which has its appearance of concreteness only after the fact, by virtue of its downfall. At least in terms of their function, the words, nailed into fixity and covered with a luminous layer of insulation, remind us of the positivistic counters. They are useful for arbitrary effect-connotations, without regard to the pathos of uniqueness which they usurp, and which itself has its orgin on the market, on that market for which what is rare has exchange value.

With the assertion of meaning at all costs, the old antisophistic emotion seeps into the so-called mass society. Ever since the victory of Plato and Aristotle over the Socratic left, that emotion has dominated the official position of philosophy. Whatever refused subjection to it was pushed off into powerless undercurrents. Only the more recent positivism has made sophistic motives reputable by its alliance with science. The jargon struggles against this alliance. Without judgment it hands down the judgment of tradition. The shame of the sophists, opposed by Plato, was the fact that they did not fight against falsity in order to change the slave society, but rather raised doubts about truth in order to arm thought for whatever was. Their kind of destruction was indeed similar to the totalitarian concept of ideology. Plato could caricature the Gorgias sophists as clowns because thought, once it has been

29. [*Klosterfrau, Jägermeister, Schänke:* established brand names of well-known liqueurs and wines.]

44

freed from concrete knowledge and the nature of the object, reduces to farce that moment of play which is essential to thought—turns such a moment into a ghost of that mimesis which is combatted by every enlightenment.[30] Nevertheless, the antisophistic movement misuses its insight into such misconstructions of free-wheeling thought—misuses them in order to discredit thought, through thought. This was the way Nietzsche criticized Kant, raising the charge of over-subtle thinking in the same tone as that adopted magisterially by Hegel, when he spoke of "reasoning." In the modish antisophistic movement there is a sad confluence: of a necessary critique of isolated instrumental reason with a grim defense of institutions against thought. The jargon, a waste product of the modern that it attacks, seeks to protect itself—along with literally destructive institutions—against the suspicion of being destructive: by simultaneously accusing other, mostly anticonservative, groups of sinful intellectuality, of that sin which lies deep in the jargon's own unnaïve, reflective principle of existence. Demagogically it uses the double character of the antisophistic. That consciousness is false which, externally, and, as Hegel says, without being in the thing, places itself above this thing and manages it from above; but criticism becomes equally ideological at the moment when it lets it be known, self-righteously, that thought must have a ground. Hegel's dialectic went beyond the doctrine that thought, in order to be true, needs some absolute starting point, free of doubt. This doctrine be-

30. Cf. Max Horkheimer and Theodor W. Adorno, *Dialektik der Aufklärung* (Amsterdam, 1947), pp. 20 ff.

comes all the more terroristic in the jargon of authenticity, as it more autocratically locates its starting point outside of the texture of thought. Antisophistic attitudes, in the final stages of processed mythology, are hardened forms of causal thinking. The relapse of the risen metaphysics, behind dialectics, is chalked up by the jargon to a return to the mothers.

> When everything has been cut off, the root lies bared. The root is the origin out of which we grew and which we have forgotten in the creepers of opinions, habits, and schemata of comprehension.[31]

Even later in *Vernunft und Existenz,* Jaspers writes:

> Only in this way could the true strength of man be realized. The power of the absolute in him, proven in every possibility of struggle and questioning, would no longer need suggestion, hate, lust for cruelty in order to become active, no longer need the intoxication of big words and ununderstood dogmas in order to believe in itself. Only that way would it actually become severe, hard and sober. Only in this way can all the self-deceptions disappear without destroying man in the process of destroying his life-lies. Only in this way will the true ground reveal itself unveiled from the depth.[32]

The authentic ones defame sophistry, but they drag its arbitrariness along in their programs, instead of prov-

31. Karl Jaspers, *Der philosophische Glaube* (Munich, 1948), p. 125. [English translation by E. B. Ashton, *Philosophical Faith and Revelation* (New York, 1967). The quotation is translated from the original German.]

32. Karl Jaspers, *Vernunft und Existenz* (Munich, 1960) pp. 98 ff. [English translation by W. Earle, *Reason and Existenz: Five Lectures* (London, 1956). The quotation is translated from the original German.]

ing to be a match for it. But they agree with the Sophists in their favorite thesis, that man alone is important—that *sententia* of *Homo mensura* warmed over again with unexpected fulsomeness. As once before, the social model of their chosen scapegoat is urban freedom, which, in the past, helped thought to emancipate itself. The only difference is the fact that in the strict rational order of bourgeois society the mobility of person and spirit are less threatening to groups, which in effect no longer exist in highly industrialized countries. But it constantly challenges the continuing irrationality of the total system, which would like to prune away what is still vegetating on from the social modes of behavior developed under liberalism.

Therefore the jargon must defend, so as not to be lost, transitory social forms which are incompatible with the contemporary state of the forces of production. If it wanted to mount the barricades itself, then it would have to engage itself not only for a position much scorned among its believers, but possibly also for that rationality which the exchange society both promises and denies, and through which that society could be transcended. The bourgeois form of rationality has always needed irrational supplements, in order to maintain itself as what it is, continuing injustice through justice. Such irrationality in the midst of the rational is the working atmosphere of authenticity. The latter can support itself on the fact that over a long period of time literal as well as figurative mobility, a main element in bourgeois equality, always turned into injustice for those who could not entirely keep up. They experienced the progress of society as a verdict:

a pawned-off remembrance of their suffering, under that system, brings authenticity, along with its jargon, to a ferment. Its bubbles cause the true object of the suffering, the particular constitution of society, to disappear. For the selected victims of the feeling against mobility have themselves been condemned, ever since the sphere of circulation was fused into the sphere of production. The jargon strives to turn the bitterness of the indigenous, of the mute, into something like a metaphysical-moral verdict of annhilation against the man who can speak out; and the jargon has had so much success only for this reason, because this verdict in question has already in effect been spoken, and has been carried out in Germany against innumerable people—because the gesture of rooted genuineness is at one with that of the historical conquerors. That is the substantial element in authenticity, the holy fount of its strength. Taciturnity and silence are the best counterpoint to existential and existentialist babble. The order which this babble aims at is itself one that reaches for speechlessness of sign and command. In happy agreement with its consumers, the jargon fills the breach created by the societally necessary disintegration of language. *Petit bourgeois* have few acquaintances; they feel uncomfortable as soon as they come together with people they don't already know, and their duplicity turns this attitude into a virtue. Not lastly, the jargon bears some resemblance to the rough manners of a doorman, in an Alpine hotel, who hectors the guests as if they were intruders, and in this way wins their trust. In face of the social stasis that once again is darkening the horizon, a shimmer of humanity is shed back onto the officiously persuasive word of the day before yesterday. If philosophy were to take back into society the experiences which were precipitated in the jargon in the false forms of its distilled essences—society being the place where they originated—and if the word "origin" had any meaning at all, then philosophy would be able to go beyond the opposition of mobility and fixity, of groundlessness and authenticity. It would then recognize these oppositions as elements of the same guilty whole, in which heroes and businessmen are of value to each other. The liberalism that hatched the culture industry produced forms of reflection that are encountered indignantly by the jargon of authenticity, although it is itself one of them. This liberalism was the ancestor of the fascism which destroyed both it and its later potential customers. But of course the blood guilt of that which echoes today, in the jargon, is incomparably greater than the deceptive maneuvers of mobility, whose principles are incompatible with those of immediate power.

Heidegger is not the matador of such political strategies, and in fact he protects himself against their blunt directness. It is true that he does use the word "authenticity" centrally in *Sein und Zeit*,[33] and most of the familiar shorthand is spread around over his best-known text—spread with gestures, of incontestable authority, which the mass of the authentics then mechanically imitate; there is unquestioned agreement about the undiscussed core of all this. In the same way Heidegger struggles to show reserve toward all the

33. Heidegger, *Being and Time*, pp. 304 ff., also pp. 68–69.

current phrases which he, with ease, can put aside as vulgar misunderstanding. Nevertheless, as soon as he loosens his voluntary self-censorship, he falls into the jargon, with a provinciality which cannot be excused on the grounds that it becomes thematic of itself. He has published a little volume of gnomic thoughts entitled *Out of the Experience of Thinking*. Its form keeps to the middle ground between poetry and pre-Socratic fragment. Yet the sibylline character of the pre-Socratic fragments really results, at least in many of them, from the accident of a discontinuous tradition, and not from secretiveness. Heidegger has praise for the "splendor of the simple." [34] He brings back the threadbare ideology of pure materials, from the realm of handicrafts to that of the mind—as if words were pure, and, as it were, roughened material. But textiles of that sort are mediated, today, through their calculated opposition to mass production; and in just that way Heidegger wants, synthetically, to create a primal sense for pure words.

Another specifically social element plays into the category of the simple: the elevation of the cheap, in accordance with the wishes of the proudly declining elite—an elevation related to youth music, which gladly goes along with the jargon and lets itself be accompanied by it. Being behind the times historically is no less eagerly converted into the feeling of the fatefully tragic, than into that of something higher; that too goes along with the silent identification of the

34. Heidegger, *Aus der Erfahrung des Denkens* (Pfullingen, 1954), p. 13.

archaic with the genuine. But the triviality of the simple is not, as Heidegger would like it to be, attributable to the value-blindness of thought that has lost being. Such triviality comes from thinking that is supposedly in tune with being and reveals itself as something supremely noble. Such triviality is the sign of that classifying thought, even in the simplest word, from which Heidegger pretends that he has escaped: namely, abstraction. Already in the first version of *Geist der Utopie*, Ernst Bloch says that symbol intentions, which are for him the traces of messianic light in the darkened world, are in fact not expressed by the most simple basic relationships and basic words, like "the old man, the mother, and death." But Heidegger, in his fastidious Humanism letter, lets us hear these words:

> Man is not the lord of existence. Man is the shepherd of being. In this "less" man loses nothing, but rather wins, by reaching the truth of Being. He wins the essential poverty of the shepherd, whose worth consists in being called, by Being itself, into the trueness of its truth. This call comes as the throwing from which the thrownness of existence stems. In his being-historical, [*seinsgeschichtlich*] essence, man is the existent whose being as ek-sistence consists in his living in the neighborhood of Being. Man is the neighbor of Being.[35]

Philosophical banality is generated when that magical participation in the absolute is ascribed to the general concept—a participation which puts the lie to that concept's conceivability.

35. Heidegger, *Über den Humanismus* (Frankfurt, 1949) p. 29.

Philosophizing, according to Heidegger, is a danger to thought.[36] But the authentic thinker, harsh toward anything so modernistic as philosophy, writes: "When in early summer isolated narcissi bloom hidden in the meadow, and the mountain rose glistens under the maple tree . . ."[37] or: "When from the slopes of the high valley, where the herds are slowly passing, the cow bells ring and ring . . ."[38] Or verses:

> The woods make camp
> the streams rush on
> the cliffs remain
> the rain runs.
> The meadows wait
> the fountains spring
> the winds dwell
> blessing takes thought.[39]

The renewing of thinking through outmoded language can be judged by these instances. The archaic is the expressive ideal of this language: "The oldest element of the old comes up behind us in our thinking and yet meets us head on."[40] But Jungnickel knows how to put it: the revenge of the myth on the person who is curious about it, on the denouncer of thinking. "The poetic character of thinking is still concealed,"[41] Heidegger adds, in order to forestall criticism at all costs: "where it shows itself, it for a long time re-

36. Heidegger, *Aus der Erfahrung*, p. 15.
37. *Ibid.*, p. 12.
38. *Ibid.*, p. 22.
39. *Ibid.*, p. 27.
40. *Ibid.*, p. 19.
41. *Ibid.*, p. 23.

sembles the utopia of a half-poetic intellect." [42] Still the half-poetic intellect which babbles forth those pieces of wisdom bears less resemblance to this, or to any other unsuccessful utopia, than to the work of some trusty folk art, which after all is not used to speaking well about those things. During the Hitler period, and we can feel with him, Heidegger turned down an academic appointment in Berlin. He justifies that in an article, "Why Do We Remain in the Province?" With wily strategy he disarms the charge that he is provincial; he uses the term "provincialism" in a positive sense. His strategy takes this form: "When on a deep winter night a wild snowstorm rages around the cabin, and covers and conceals everything, then the time is ripe for philosophy. Its question must then become simple and essential." [43] Whether questions are essential can in any case only be judged by the answers given; there is no way of anticipating, and certainly not by the criterion of a simplicity based on meteorological events. That simplicity says as little about truth as about its opposite; Kant, Hegel were as complicated and as simple as their content forced them to be. But Heidegger insinuates a preestablished harmony between essential content and homey murmuring. Therefore, the echoes of Jungnickel here are not just loveable lapses. They are there to deafen any suspicion that the philosopher might be an intellectual: "And philosophical work does not take place as the

42. *Ibid.*
43. Quoted in Guido Schneeberger, *Nachlese zu Heidegger, Dokumente zu seinem Leben und Denken* (Bern, 1962), p. 216.

spare-time activity of a crank. It belongs right in the midst of the labor of farmers." [44] One would like at least to know the farmers' opinion about that. Heidegger does not need their opinion. For "during the time of the evening work-pause, he sits, on the stove bench along with the farmers . . . or at the table in the corner, under the crucifix, and then we usually don't talk at all. We smoke our pipes in silence." [45] "One's own work's inner belonging, to the Black Forest and its people, comes from a century-long Germanic-Swabian rootedness, which is irreplaceable." [46] After all, Heidegger says it himself. Johann Peter Hebel, who comes from the same region, and to whom Heidegger would like to give the place of honor on the mantelpiece, hardly ever appealed to this rootedness; instead he passed on his greetings to the peddlers Scheitele and Nausel, in one of the most beautiful pieces of prose in defense of the Jews that was ever written in German.[47] Rootedness, however, puffs itself up:

Recently I got a second invitation to the University of Berlin. On such an occasion I leave the city and go back to my cabin. I hear what the mountains and woods and farmyards say. On the way I drop in on my old friend, a seventy-five-year-old farmer. He has read in the newspaper about the Berlin invitation. What will he say? He slowly presses the sure glance of his clear eyes against mine, holds his mouth tightly closed, lays his faithful and cautious hand on my shoulder—and almost im-

44. *Ibid.*
45. *Ibid.*, p. 217.
46. *Ibid.*
47. Cf. Johann Peter Hebel, *Werke* (Berlin, 1874) II, 254.

54

perceptibly shakes his head. That means: absolutely No! [48]

While the philosopher complains to other Blubo-friends about their advertising of the Blubo,[49] which would be detrimental to his monopoly, his reflected unreflectiveness degenerates into chummy chit-chat, for the sake of the rural setting with which he wants to stand on a confidential footing. The description of the old farmer reminds us of the most washed-out clichés in plough-and-furrow novels, from the region of a Frenssen; and it reminds us equally of the praise of being silent, which the philosopher authorizes not only for his farmers but also for himself. Here we find an ignorance of everything we have learned about rural people: for instance in French realism from Balzac's late work to Maupassant; from a literature not attuned to the musty instincts of German *petit-bourgeois* kitsch; from a literature which would be available in translation even to a pre-Socratic. The small farmer owes his continuing existence entirely to gracious gifts from that exchange society by which his very ground and foundation, even in appearance, have been removed; in the face of this exchange the farmers have nothing on their horizon except something worse—the immediate exploitation of the family without which they would be bankrupt: this hollowed-out state, the perpetual crisis of the small farmer's business, has its echo in the hollowness of the jargon. The subsidies which are

48. Schneeberger, *Nachlese*, p. 218.
49. [*Blubo*: catchword of the Nazi movement, emphasizing the interdependence of one's life with one's native soil. A provincial version of *pro patria mori*.]

paid to the small farmers are the very ground of that which the primal words of the jargon add to that which in fact they mean. Like less prominent *porte-paroles* of authenticity, Heidegger is filled with the disdainful pride of inwardness, which he touches on philosophically, in his thought about Hegel's critique of it.[50] Whoever is forced by the nature of his work to stay in one place, gladly makes a virtue out of necessity. He tries to convince himself and others that his bound-ness is of a higher order. The financially threatened farmer's bad experiences with middlemen substantiate this opinion. The socially clumsy person who may be partially excluded from society hates those middlemen as jacks of all trades. This hatred joins with resistance against all agents, from the cattle dealer to the journalist. In 1956 the stable professions, which are themselves a stage of social development, are still the norms for Heidegger. He praises them in the name of a false eternity of agrarian conditions: "Man tries in vain to bring the globe to order through planning, when he is not in tune with the consoling voice of the country lane." [51] North America knows no country lanes, not even villages. Philosophy, which is ashamed of its name, needs the sixth-hand symbol of the farmer as a proof of its primalness, as a way of acquiring some otherwise unavailable distinctiveness. However, Lessing's insight still applies, as it did in his time: the insight that the aesthetic critic does not need to do better himself than what he criticizes. That which

50. Cf. Heidegger, *Being and Time*, pp. 248 ff.
51. Heidegger, *Der Feldweg* (Frankfurt, 1956) p. 4.

was right for the *Hamburg Dramaturgy* is also reasonable for philosophical theory: the self-awareness of its limitations does not obligate it to authentic poetic creation. But it must have the power to prevent thinking people from producing mere aesthetic staples; otherwise, these argue against a philosophy which pretends to scorn arguments as confusing. Its noble philistinism grows into the jargon of authenticity.

As in this jargon, and even in Heidegger, the evidence of language reveals the falsity of rootedness— at least as soon as rootedness descends to something that has a concrete content. Heidegger works with an antithesis between being alone and loneliness:

> City people are often surprised by the farmers' long, monotonous state of being alone among the mountains. Yet it is not being alone, but rather loneliness. In big cities man can easily be alone as it is hardly possible to be elsewhere. But he can never be lonely there. For loneliness has that primal power not of isolating us, but of casting all existence free into the wide nearness of the essence of all things.[52]

However things may stand with this distinction, in terms of content, language, to which Heidegger is turning for testimony, does not know the present distinction in the present form. The Electra monologue of Hofmannsthal, who certainly understood such nuances, begins: "Alone, all alone." The human condition of the heroine is, if anything at all, that ultimate being-thrown-back-on-oneself in which Heidegger trusts, somewhat optimistically. He relies on the way that

52. Quoted in Schneeberger, *Nachlese,* p. 217.

state leads "into the wide nearness of the essence of all things"; though in fact such situations are no less likely to force people into obsessive narrowness and impoverishment. Looked at the other way around—in opposition to Heidegger—language will rather suggest that people are lonely in big cities or on public holidays, but that they cannot be alone on such occasions. In any case present usage is indecisive on this matter. Heidegger's philosophy, which takes so much advantage of its ability to listen, renders itself deaf to words. The emphatic nature of this philosophy arouses the belief that it fits itself into the words, while it is only a cover for arbitrariness. Heidegger's primal sounds ape—as such sounds usually do. Of course, even a more sensitive linguistic organ than his would hardly accomplish anything better in this matter in which he fails. Every such effort has its linguistically logical limit in the accidental element of even the most precise word. Words' own meanings weigh heavily in them. But these words do not use themselves up in their meanings: they themselves are caught up in their context. This fact is underestimated in the high praise given to science by every pure analysis of meaning, starting with Husserl's; especially by that of Heidegger, which considers itself far above science. Only that person satisfies the demand of language who masters the relation of language to individual words in their configurations. Just as the fixing of the pure element of meaning threatens to pass over into the arbitrary, so the belief in the primacy of the configurative threatens to pass into the badly functional, the merely communicative—into scorn for the objective aspect of words. In language that is worth something both of these elements are transmitted.

Allegedly hale life is opposed to damaged life, on whose societalized consciousness, on whose "malaise," the jargon speculates. Through the ingrained language form of the jargon, that hale life is equated with agrarian conditions, or at least with simple commodity economy, far from all social considerations. This life is in effect equated to something undivided, protectingly closed, which runs its course in a firm rhythm and unbroken continuity. The field of association here is a left-over of romanticism and is transplanted without second thought into the contemporary situation, to which it stands in harsher contradiction than ever before. In that situation the categories of the jargon are gladly brought forward, as though they were not abstracted from generated and transitory situations, but rather belonged to the essence of man, as inalienable possibility. Man is the ideology of dehumanization. Conclusions are drawn from certain categories which remind us of somewhat primal social relationships, where the institutions of exchange do not yet have complete power over the relationships of men. From those categories it is concluded that their core, man, is immediately present among contemporary men, that he is there to realize his *eidos*. Past forms of societalization, prior to the division of labor, are surreptitiously adopted as if they were eternal. Their reflection falls upon later conditions which have already been victimized by progressive rationalization, and in contrast to those the earlier states seem the more human. That which authentics of lesser rank call with gusto the image of man, they locate in a zone in which it is no longer permitted to ask from where those conditions emerged; neither can one ask what was done to the subjugated at any particular time, with the transition from nomadic life to settledness—nor what was done to those who can no longer move around; nor whether the undivided condition itself, both unconscious and compulsive, did not breed and earn its own downfall. The talk about man makes itself popular in the old-fashioned, half-timbered, gable-roof way. But it also wins friends in a more contemporary way, in the gesture of a radicalism which wants to dismantle whatever merely conceals, and which concerns itself with the naked essence that hides under all cultural disguises. However, as it is a question of Man and not, for the sake of men, of the conditions which are made by men and which harden into opposition against them, we are released from criticizing them, as though, temporally bound like its object, such a critique were all too shallow. This position fundamentally suppresses the motif of the Kantian "Idea toward a General History from a Cosmopolitan Point of View": the idea that states of affairs worthy of Man can only be produced through antagonism, from out of their own force, not from a pure idea. The talk about man is so worthless because it prepares for untruth that which is of highest truth. There is great stress on the existential elements of man, in which slack and self-surfeited thought thinks it holds, in its hands, that concretion which it has lost through its transformation into method. Such maneuvers simply deflect us from seeing how little it is here a question of man, who has been condemned to the status of an appendage. The expression of the word "man" has itself modified its form historically. In the expressionistic literature since the period of the First World War, the word "man" has had a historical value—thanks to the protest against that flagrant inhumanity which found human material for matériel slaughter. The honorable old reification of bourgeois society, which comes into its own in the great periods, and is called individual human effort, in that way becomes graspable; and, in that way, antagonistically, also becomes its own counter-concept. The sentence "Man is good" was false, but at least it needed no metaphysical-anthropological sauce. It is already different with the expressionistic "O Man," a manifesto directed against that which, done only by men, is a usurpatory positing. The expressionistic "O Man" was already inclined to leave men's violence out of consideration. The undisputed, childlike sense of universal humanity taints itself with that which it opposes—as could be shown in the writings of Franz Werfel. The jargon's image of man, meanwhile, is still the selling-out of that uninhibited "O Man," and the negative truth concerning it.

To characterize the change in function of the word "man," we need only consider two titles which resemble one another. At the time of the German November Revolution, there appeared a book by the pacifist Ludwig Rubiner, *Man in the Middle;* in the fifties, a book called *Man at the Center of the Business Operation.* Thanks to its abstractness, the concept lets itself be squirted like grease into the same machinery it once wanted to assail. Its pathos, meanwhile evaporated, still echoes in the ideology which holds that business, which must be operated by men, exists for their sake. This means that the organization has to take care of its workers so that their productivity will climb. Like Elsie, the happy American advertisement-cow, that phrase about Man, whom the phrase enjoins us to care for, would not be so convincing if the phrase did not rely on a suspicion; the suspicion that, after all, the overpowering conditions of society really were made by men and can be undone by them. The overpowering strength of those relationships, like that of myth, has in it an element of fetishism and mere appearance. Just as the in-itself of the institution is mere appearance, a reflection of petrified human states of affairs, so in reality this appearance dominates men to the same degree. This is what debases the appeal to an inalienable essence of Man which has long been alienated. It was not Man who created the institutions but particular men in a particular constellation with nature and with themselves. This constellation forced the institutions on them in the same way that men erected those institutions, without consciousness. All that was formulated incisively during the Vormärz, particularly by Marx, against Feuerbach's anthropology and the young Hegelians. Both appearance and necessity are elements of the world of wares. Cognition fails as soon as it isolates one of these elements. He who accepts the world of wares as the in-itself, which it pretends to be, is deceived by the mechanisms which Marx analyzed in the chapter on fetishes. He who neglects this in-itself, the value of exchange, as mere illusion, gives in to the ideology of universal humanity. He clings to forms of an immediate togetherness, which are historically irretrievable if in fact they ever existed in any other form. Once capitalism has grown uneasy about theoretical self-assertion, its advocates prefer to use the categories of spontaneous life in order to present what is man-made. They present those categories as if they were valid now and here. The jargon busily splashes beyond all this, perhaps even proud of its historical obliviousness—as if this obliviousness were already the humanly immediate.

The angel's voices with which the jargon registers the word "Man," are derived by the jargon from the doctrine of man as the image of God. The word "Man" sounds all the more irrefutable and persuasive the more it seals itself off against its theological origin. Some element in it points back to a linguistic phenomenon drawn from the *Jugendstil,* an element which the jargon has prepared for mass consumption. The link in the history of philosophy between the *Jugendstil* and the jargon is probably the youth movement. For one of his plays Hauptmann chose the title *Solitary Men.* In a novel by Countess Reventlow, a professor is ridiculed who belonged to the costume-party *bohème* of Munich around 1910. He says, about every person whom he considers fit to enter the Schwabing circle, "What a wonderful man." This is related to the mannerism of actors, from the early Reinhardt era, who would place their hands on their hearts, would open their eyes as wide as they could, and would in general dramatize themselves. Once the original theological image has fallen, transcendence, which in the great religions is separated from the likeness by power-

ful taboos—thou shalt have no graven images of me—
is shifted to the likeness. This image is then said to be
full of wonder, since wonders no longer exist. Here
all the concretion of authenticity has its mystery: the
concreteness of whatever is as its own image. While
there is nothing more to which wonderful man has to
bow down, man who is said to be wonderful because he
is nothing but man, the jargon acts as man should
once have acted before the Godhead. The jargon aims
at a humility which is unquestioned and without relation. Such humility is presented as human virtue-in-
itself. From the outset such humility has gone well
with the insolence of the self-positing subject. The
hiddenness of that which humility aims at, is in itself
an invitation to be celebrated. This element has long
been present in the concept of reverence, even in
Goethe's understanding of it. Jaspers expressly recommends reverence, independent of its object. He condemns its absence and easily finds his way to the hero
cult without being frightened by Carlyle's example.

> In the vision of historical figures of human greatness,
> the strength of reverence holds fast the measure of
> man's essence, and of his potential. Reverence does not
> allow the destruction of what it has seen. It remains
> true to what was effective as tradition in its own self-
> becoming. Reverence grasps the origin of its substance
> in those individual men in whose shadow reverence be-
> came conscious. In the form of unyielding piety it still
> maintains its preserving function. What no longer has
> reality in the world remains present in reverence as an
> absolute claim, by means of memory.[53]

53. Jaspers, *Die geistige Situation,* p. 170.

In the jargon, however, the word "Man" no longer relies on human dignity as idealism, in spite of the cult
of historical figures and of greatness in itself. Instead,
man is to have his powerlessness and nothingness as
his substance; this becomes a theme in the philosophers in question. This powerlessness and nothingness
of man is coming close to its realization in present
society. Such a historical state of affairs is then trans-
posed into the pure essence of Man. It becomes affirmed and eternalized at the same time. In this way
the jargon plunders the concept of Man, who is to be
sublime because of his nothingness. It robs him of precisely those traits which have, as their content, the
criticism of states of affairs which preclude the divine
rights of the soul. This criticism has been immanent in
all enlightenment, as well as in early German idealism.
The jargon goes hand in hand with a concept of Man
from which all memory of natural law has been eradicated. Yet as an invariable, in the jargon man himself
becomes something like a supernatural nature-cate-
gory. Previously, the unbearable transience of a false
and unsatisfied life was counteracted by theology,
which gave hope of an eternal life. This hope disappears in the praise of the transient as absolute, a praise
which of course Hegel had already deigned to bestow.
As it runs in the jargon: suffering, evil, and death are
to be accepted, not to be changed. The public is being
trained in this tour de force of maintaining a balance.
They are learning to understand their nothingness as
Being, to revere actual, avoidable, or at least corrigible
need as the most humane element in the image of Man.
They are learning to respect authority in itself because

of their innate human insufficiency. Although such authority now rarely calls itself god-sent, it still holds on to the regal insignia which once it borrowed from God the father. Insofar as this authority no longer has any legitimation, apart from merely being there, blind and obscure, it becomes radically evil. This is the reason why the universally human language-gesture is in good standing with the totalitarian state. In the view of absolute power subjects are indifferent to this language-gesture—in the double sense of indifferent. The Third Reich, which could present such considerable majorities that it was hardly necessary to forge the election returns, was once credited by Hjalmar Schacht as the true democracy. He is confirmed by the jargon's view of Man, which was at times more innocent. According to the latter view, all men are equal in their powerlessness, in which they possess being. Humanity becomes the most general and empty form of privilege. It is strictly suited to a form of consciousness which no longer suffers any privileges yet which still finds itself under the spell of privilege. Such universal humanity, however, is ideology. It caricatures the equal rights of everything which bears a human face, since it hides from men the unalleviated discriminations of societal power: the differences between hunger and overabundance, between spirit and docile idiocy. Chastely moved, man lets himself be addressed through Man: it doesn't cost anyone anything. But whoever refuses this appeal gives himself over as non-human to the administrators of the jargon, and can be sacrificed by them, if such a sacrifice is needed. For he, the non-human, and not the institution of power, is the one whose pride tramples human dignity into the dirt. In the mask of the jargon any self-interested action can give itself the air of public interest, of service to Man. Thus, nothing is done in any serious fashion to alleviate men's suffering and need. Self-righteous humanity, in the midst of a general inhumanity, only intensifies the inhuman state of affairs. This is a state of affairs which necessarily remains hidden to those who suffer here and now. The jargon only doubles the hiding cover. The compensation and consolation offered by the jargon and its world are standardized by their twisted desire for that which they are refused.

The empty phrase, Man, distorts man's relation to his society as well as the content of what is thought in the concept of Man. The phrase does not bother about the real division of the subject into separated functions that cannot be undone by the voice of mere spirit. The so-called Platonic psychology already expresses the internalization of the societal division of labor. Each function within the person, once firmly defined, negates the person's total principle. The person becomes simply the sum of his functions. In the face of this situation, however, the person becomes all the worse, since his own laboriously gained unity has remained fragile. Each individual function, created under the law of self-preservation, becomes so firmly congealed that none can exist by itself, that no life can be constructed out of its functional pieces. The individual functions turn against the self which they are supposed to serve. Life, insofar as it still exists, indicts such separation as false—for example in the verbal separation among thinking, feeling, and desiring. No thought is a thought—or more than a tautology—that does not also desire something. Without an element of cognition, no feeling and no will can be more than a fleeting motion. It is easy for the jargon to point its finger at the silliness of this division; for in the meantime it has swallowed the current term "alienation." The jargon, for example, was only too willing to grant depth to the young Marx, in order to be able to escape the critic of political economy. In this process the real force of the splitting of the individual subject is lost from view. The thought that testifies to this split suddenly finds itself vituperated. The unsatisfiable triumph, won again over the mechanistic psychology of the nineteenth century, misuses the insight of Gestalt theory, which itself is no longer quite dewy fresh—misuses that insight as pretext for not having to touch on that which is felt to be the wound. The progress of science, which otherwise is not much admired, and which did not take place in precisely this situation, is viewed as the reason not to consider the wound. The authentics shun Freud by exulting in the fact that they are more modern than Freud, but without any reason. Meanwhile, in a timely fashion, the fulsome talk about the whole man rooted in being is put into its place by psychoanalysis. No elevation of the concept of Man has any power in the face of his actual degradation into a bundle of functions. The only help lies in changing the conditions which brought the state of affairs to this point—conditions which uninterruptedly reproduce themselves on a larger scale. By means of the magic formula of existence, one dis-

68

regards society, and the psychology of real individuals which is dependent on that society. Thus one insists on the changing of Man, who in Hegel's sense exists merely in the abstract. This results only in a tightening of the reins—not in elevation but in the continuing of the old suppressing ideology. While the authentics attack psychoanalysis, they are really aiming at instinct. The degradation of instinct is taken over unreflectedly into their ethics. Thus Jaspers says:

> The exclusiveness in the love of the sexes unconditionally binds two people for the entire future. Without being able to be grounded, this love rests in the decision which tied the self to this loyalty, at the moment in which it came to itself authentically through the other. To renounce what is negative—polygamous erotic activity—is the consequence of a positive element. This positive element is only true, in the form of a present love, when it includes the whole life. The negative element, the will not to throw oneself away, is the result of an absolute willingness for this loyalty; willingness exercised by means of the possibility of self-realization. There is no self-realization without strictness in eroticism. Eroticism becomes humanly meaningful only in the exclusiveness of unconditioned commitment.[54]

"Commitment" is the current word for the unreasonable demand of discipline. The term "commitment" unites Heidegger and Jaspers together with the lowest *tractatus*-writers. At first the term was designed to naturalize a loan word. Chewing their cuds, patriotic pedagogues would say that commitment was actually the name of religion. But it was not only the exaggera-

54. *Ibid.*, p. 171.

tion of German ways that allowed for the naturalization of "commitments." The loan-word "religion" demanded subordination to something definite: Christian revelation or the divine law of the Jews. This element is no longer felt in the newly coined "commitment." The expression gives the appearance of reviving that sensual concretion which had become effaced in the loan word. But, in contrast to that sensuous color, the element to which the concretion adhered has become obscured. People now dress up the factual state of commitment. The concept preserves the authority whose source of origin is cut off right from the beginning. The thing that is understood under the term "commitment" is no better than the word. Commitments are offered not for their own truth but as a medicine against nihilism, in the same manner as the values which were current a generation before, and which surreptitiously circulate again today. Commitments are classed under mental hygiene and, for that reason, undermine the transcendence which they prescribe. The campaign that the jargon is launching records one Pyrrhic victory after another. The genuineness of need and belief, which is questionable anyway, has to turn itself into the criterion for what is desired and believed; and in this way it becomes no longer genuine. This is the reason why no one can say the word "genuineness" without becoming ideological. Nietzsche still used the term in an anti-ideological way. In the jargon, however, it stands out in the unending mumble of the liturgy of inwardness. Like a ragpicker, the jargon usurps the final protesting movements of a subject which in its downfall is thrown back on itself and hucksters those movements off. The edge is removed from the living subject's protest against being condemned to play roles. The American theory of role-playing is so popular because it flattens out this protest into the structure of society. And the subject is told that the force from which he flees back into his cave has no power over him. Not lastly, the jargon is sacred as the language of an invisible kingdom, which exists only in the obsessive folly of the silent majority. So as not to scatter oneself—today, through the consumer market—it is removed from its social context and interpreted as something which is of essence. But in that way it only negotiates something negative. *Petits-bourgeois* watch over *petits-bourgeois*. Dispersion, which is the consequence of the consumer habit, is viewed as original evil. Consciousness, however, has already been disowned in the sphere of production, which trains individuals to disperse themselves.

Heidegger depicts the authentic state in contrast to the dispersed one:

> The Self of everyday *Dasein* is the *they-self*, which we distinguish from the *authentic Self*—that is, from the Self which has been taken hold of in its own way. . . . As they-self, the particular Dasein has been *dispersed* into the "they," and must first find itself. This dispersal characterizes the "subject" of that kind of Being which we know as concernful absorption in the world we encounter as closest to us.[55]

He does not think of the connection between the large urban center, of high capitalism and that dispersion which was noted by Georg Simmel and already felt by

55. Heidegger, *Being and Time*, p. 167.

Baudelaire. Whatever remains solely by itself, as one's authentic existence, becomes no less impoverished than that which dissolves into situations. Both Hegel and Goethe experienced and criticized inwardness as a merely accidental element. They saw it as the condition for right consciousness, and as an element which had to be negated because of its limitation. The memory of this criticism has been sublimated, since nonmind has accomplished so much more thoroughly what the mind once demanded of the mind.

The reconciliation between the inner and outer worlds, which Hegelian philosophy still hoped for, has been postponed ad infinitum. Thus it has become unnecessary to advocate alienation, since the latter is in power anyway, as the law of those who are happy extroverts. At the same time the consciousness of the rupture becomes more and more unbearable. For slowly this rupture changes self-consciousness into self-deception. Ideology can grasp onto the fact that the growing powerlessness of the subject, its secularization, was at the same time a loss of world and concreteness. With good reason, the first original philosophy after Hegel, that of Kierkegaard, has been called a philosophy of inwardness. But this very Kierkegaardian philosophy has rid itself of the notion of a real innerworldly reconciliation. The reflection on inwardness, the positing of it together with an element of its becoming, points to its real abolition. The jargon brought into circulation many of the categories of inwardness and thus contributed its part to the destruction of inwardness by means of such a contradiction. After the failure of the bourgeois revolution in Germany, the history of inwardness became, from its first day on, the history of its downfall. The less powerful the subject becomes, the more the sphere, which once self-consciously confessed itself to be inwardness, shrinks to an abstract point; the greater becomes the temptation for inwardness to proclaim itself and throw itself onto that same market by which it is terrified. Terminologically, inwardness becomes a value and a possession behind which it entrenches itself; and it is surreptitiously overcome by reification. It becomes Kierkegaard's nightmare of the "aesthetic world" of the mere onlooker, whose counterpart is to be the existential inwardly man. Whatever wants to remain absolutely pure from the blemish of reification is pasted onto the subject as a firm attribute. Thus the subject becomes an object in the second degree, and finally the mass product of consolation: from that found in Rilke's "Beggars can call you brother and still you can be a king" to the notorious poverty which is the great inward gleam of the spirit.

Those philosophers like Hegel and Kierkegaard, who testified to the unhappy state of consciousness for itself, understood inwardness in line with Protestant tradition: essentially as negation of the subject, as repentance. The inheritors who, by sleight of hand, changed unhappy consciousness into a happy non-dialectic one, preserve only the limited self-righteousness which Hegel sensed a hundred years before fascism. They cleanse inwardness of that element which contains its truth, by eliminating self-reflection, in which the ego becomes transparent to itself as a piece of the world. Instead, the ego posits itself as higher than the world and becomes subjected to the world precisely because of this. The hardened inward-

ness of today idolizes its own purity, which has supposedly been blemished by ontic elements. At least in
this regard the outset of contemporary ontology coincides with the cult of inwardness. The retreat of
ontology from the course of the world is also a retreat
from the empirical content of subjectivity. In a clas-
sically enlightened attitude, Kant took an antagonistic
stance toward the concept of the inward and separated out the empirical subject, which was dealt with
by psychology, as one thing among others.[56] He distinguished it from the transcendental subject, and subsumed it under the category of causality. With a reverse stress this is followed by the pathos of the inward
ones. They take pleasure in their scorn for psychology
without, in the manner of Kant, sacrificing to transcendental universality its alleged footing within the
individual person. They cash in on the profit of both,
so to speak. The taboos of the inward ones, which result from their animosity toward instinctual drives,
become more rigid by virtue of the fact that the subject
becomes an element of externality—by virtue of its
psychological determination.

These taboos especially rage in Jaspers' books.[57]
But in the suppression of real satisfaction, in the
transposition of satisfaction into a mere inner one,
where the self satisfies the self, all of the authentics,
even the early Heidegger, coincide. He too includes the

56. Cf. Immanuel Kant, *Kritik der reinen Verunft*, B 332 f.
(*Die Amphibolie der Reflexionsbegriffe*). [English translation
by N. K. Smith, *Critique of Pure Reason* (New York, 1965).]
57. Cf. Jaspers, *Psychologie der Weltanschauungen*, 3d ed.
(Berlin, 1925), pp. 132 ff.

term "pleasure capacity" under the categories of inauthenticity,[58] and in *Sein und Zeit* he affirms Jaspers'
statement that a psychology of world-views is by no
means a psychology.[59] The no-less-disgusting practice
of psychoanalytic language, hammering "enjoyment
capacity" into its patients without regard for what is
to be enjoyed, is simply turned upside down. But if
inwardness is neither an existent thing nor an aspect
—no matter how general—of the subject, then it turns
into an imaginary quantity. If every existent thing,
even the psychic, is cut out from the subject, then the
remainder is no less abstract than the transcendental
subject in respect to which the individual's inwardness,
as existent, imagines itself so superior. In the classic
texts of existentialism, as in that of the Kierkegaardian sickness unto death, existence becomes a relationship to itself, under which heading nothing further
can be conceived. It becomes, as it were, an absolutized
moment of mediation, without any regard for what is
mediated; and it pronounces a verdict, from the very
beginning, against any philosophy of inwardness. In
the jargon, finally, there remains from inwardness
only the most external aspect, that thinking oneself
superior which marks people who elect themselves:
the claim of people who consider themselves blessed
simply by virtue of being what they are. Without any
effort, this claim can turn into an elitist claim, or into
a readiness to attach itself to elites which then quickly
gives the ax to inwardness. A symptom of the transfor-

58. Heidegger, *Being and Time*, p. 68.
59. *Ibid.*, p. 293, and especially pp. 348 ff.

mation of inwardness is the belief of innumerable people that they belong to an extraordinary family. The jargon of authenticity, which sells self-identity as something higher, projects the exchange formula onto that which imagines that it is not exchangeable; for as a biological individual each man resembles himself. That is what is left over after the removal of soul and immortality from the immortal soul.

The over-all appearance of the immediate, which comes to a head in inwardness—now merely a specimen—makes it unusually hard for those who are steadily exposed to the jargon to see through it. In its second-hand primalness they actually find something like contact, comparable to the feeling in the fraudulent National Socialist *Volk*-community which led people to believe that all kindred comrades are cared for and none is forgotten: permanent metaphysical subvention. The social basis for this is clear. Many instances of mediation in the market economy, which have strengthened the consciousness of alienation, are put aside in the transition to a planned economy; the routes between the whole and atomized individual subjects are shortened, as if the two extremes were near to one another. The technical progress of the means of communication runs parallel to this. These means—especially radio and television—reach the people at large in such a way that they notice none of the innumerable technical intermediations; the voice of the announcer resounds in the home, as though he were present and knew each individual. The announcers' technically and psychologically created artificial language—the model of which is the repellently confidential " 'Til we meet again"—is of the same stripe as the jargon of authenticity. The catch-word for all this is "encounter": "The book lying before us, which concerns itself with Jesus, is of a very unusual kind. It does not intend to be a biography, a 'Life of Jesus,' in the usual sense, but to lead us to an existential encounter with Jesus . . ." [60] Gottfried Keller, the lyricist, on whom the apostles of harmony looked down condescendingly, wrote a poem called "Encounter," a poem of wonderful clumsiness.[61] The poet unexpectedly meets, in the woods, her

> whom alone my heart longs for,
> wrapped whitely in scarf and hat,
> transformed by a golden shine.
> She was alone; yet I greeted her
> hardly made shy in passing on,
> because I had never seen her so
> noble, still, and beautiful.

The misty light is that of sadness, and from it the word "encounter" receives its power. But this sadness gathers to itself the feeling of departure, which is powerful and incapable of unmediated expression; it designates nothing other than, quite literally, the fact that the two people met each other without any intention. What the jargon has accomplished with the word "encounter," and what can never again be repaired,

60. *Archiv für Literaturwissenschaft*, 1960, on Rudolf Bultmann, *Jesus.*

61. Cf. Bruno Russ, *Das Problem des Todes in der Lyrik Gottfried Kellers,* Ph.D. diss. (Frankfurt a. M., 1959), pp. 189 ff., 200 ff.

does more harm to Keller's poem than a factory ever did to a landscape. "Encounter" is alienated from its literal content and is practically made usable through the idealizing of that content. There are scarcely encounters like Keller's any longer—at the most there are appointments made by telephone—in a society in which it is essentially accidental when men get to know one another; and in which what one once simply called "life" constantly melts away more and more, and, where it maintains itself at all, is considered something to be merely tolerated. But for precisely this reason encounter is praised, language has smeared organized contacts with luminous paint, because the light has gone out. The accompanying speech-gesture is that of eye-to-eye, as is the way with dictators. Whoever looks deep into somebody's eye is hoping to hypnotize him, to win power over him, and always with a threat: Are you really faithful to me? no betrayer? no Judas? Psychological interpretation of the jargon should discover in this language-gesture an unconscious homosexual transference, and should in that way also be able to explain the patriarch's eager rejection of psychoanalysis. The manic eye-to-eye glance is related to racial insanity; it wants a conspiratorial community, the feeling that we are of the same kind; it strengthens endogamy. The very desire to purify the word "encounter," and to reinstate it through strict usage, would become, through unavoidable tacit agreement, a basic element of the jargon, along with purity and primalness—an element of that jargon from which it would like to escape. What was done to "encounter" satisfies a specific need. Those encounters which counteract themselves because they are organized, those encounters to which good will, busy-body behavior and canny desire for power tirelessly exhort us, are simply covers for spontaneous actions that have become impossible. People console themselves, or are being consoled, by thinking that something has already been done about what is oppressing them when they talk about it. Conversation, after having been a means of becoming clear about something, becomes an end in itself and a substitute for that which, in terms of its sense, should follow from it. The surplus in the word "encounter"—the suggestion that something essential is already occurring when those ordered to gather converse together—that surplus has the same deception at its center as the speculation on being helped in the word "concern." Once that word meant a sickness. The jargon falls back on that: as though the individual's interest were at the same time his trouble. It begs for *caritas* but at the same time, for the sake of its human essence, it exercises terror. Here one is expected to understand a transcendental power which requires that one, again according to the jargon, should "perceive" the concern. The archaic superstition, which is still exploited today by the epistolary formula "hoping not to have asked in vain" is taken on existential RPM's by the jargon; readiness to help being, as it were, squeezed out of being.

The counterpart to that—something over which the authentics have unquestioningly grown indignant —would be communicative usage as it is found in America. "Being cooperative" means, in that context, to offer one's services to the other without remuneration, or at least to put one's time at the other's disposal in the expectation—no matter how vague—that all that will someday be repaid, since all men need all men. The German concern, however, evolved from the capitalist exchange principle at a stage in which this principle was still dominant, while the liberal norm of equivalence had been shattered. So dynamic is the linguistic character of the jargon as a whole: in it that becomes disgusting which was by no means always so.[62] In the encounters where the jargon prattles, and of which it prattles, it sides with that which it accuses by the word "encounter," namely, the over-administered world. It accommodates itself to that world through a ritual of non-accommodation. Even the Hitler dictatorship wooed for consensus; it was here that it checked its mass basis. Finally, the self-employed administration wants at every moment, under the conditions of formal democracy, to prove that it exists for the sake of the administrated whole. Therefore she makes eyes at the jargon, and it at her, the already irrational, self-sufficient authority.

The jargon proves itself as a piece of the negative spirit of the time; it institutes socially useful work within the tendency already observed by Max Weber; the tendency for administrations to expand out over

62. The author's own work taught him about the change in function. Nothing in the *Philosophie der neuen Musik*, which was written when he was still in America, warned him against "concern." Only a German critique pointed out to him the bigotry of the word. Even he who detests the jargon cannot be safe from its contagion. For this reason one should fear it all the more.

what they consider as their cultural domain. There are countless occasions on which administrators, specialists trained in law or in management, feel themselves obliged to speak, as it were, about the content of art, science, and philosophy. They are afraid of being boring, of being dry, and they would like to show their alliance with a kindred specialized spirit, though without being involved too greatly with the other in their activity and experience. If an *Oberstadtdirektor* addresses a congress of philosophers, whose own guiding principle is already as administration-oriented as the title *Oberstadtdirektor*, then he must use whatever cultural stuffing offers itself to him. And that is the jargon. This shelters him from the disagreeable task of expressing himself seriously on the matter at hand, about which he knows nothing. At the same time perhaps he can thus feign general acquaintance with the subject. The jargon is so appropriate for that because, by its very nature, it always unites the appearance of an absent concreteness with the ennobling of that concreteness. If there were no functional need for the jargon, which is hostile to function, it would hardly have become a second language—that of the languageless and those alien to language. The jargon, which is not responsible to any reason, urges people higher simply through its simultaneously standardized tone; it reproduces on the level of mind the curse which bureaucracy exercises in reality. It could be described as an ideological replica of the paralyzing quality of official functions. Their horror is made present to us by Kafka's dry language, which is itself a complete contrary to the jargon. Society's regulatory violence becomes crassly tangible to the people when they are obliged to request something from the inaccessible mouthpieces of the administration. Like these mouthpieces, the jargon speaks directly to them without letting them respond. In addition it talks them into thinking that the man behind the counter is really the man whom his name plate, recently introduced, presents him as being. Latently, the salvation formulas of the jargon are those of power, borrowed from the administrative and legal hierarchy of authority.

The bureaucratic language, seasoned with authenticity, is therefore no merely decadent form of the appropriate philosophical language, but is already preformed in the most notable texts of that philosophy. Heidegger's favorite "first of all," that has its roots as much in didactic procedure as in a Cartesian first-and-then, leads thoughts along on a leash, in the spirit of philosophical systematization; as if in a business agendum, one adjourns whatever is out of order, by the throttling schema, "but before we . . . further fundamental investigations have to be undertaken":

> This chapter, in which we shall undertake the explication of Being-in as such (that is to say of the Being of the "there") breaks up into two parts: A. the existential Constitution of the "there"; B. the everyday Being of the "there," and the falling of Dasein.[63]

Such pedantry still propagandizes for an allegedly radical philosophical reflection, which it presents as a solid science. The pedantry, in addition, is repaid by a

63. Heidegger, *Being and Time*, p. 171.

side result: that it simply never arrives at what philosophy promises. That all goes back to Husserl, in the course of whose extensive preliminary considerations one easily forgets the main thing—though critical reflection would first come to grips with the very *philosophemes* that fastidiousness pushes along in front of it. But even the assertion that practical consequences are contemptible, which has its distinguished prehistory in German idealism, cannot do without the cleverness of strategy. The administrative offices, in Kafka's world, similarly shirk decisions, which then, ungrounded, suddenly catch up with their victims. The reciprocity of the personal and apersonal in the jargon; the apparent humanization of the thingly; the actual turning of man into thing: all this is the luminous copy of that administrative situation in which both abstract justice and objective procedural orders appear under the guise of face-to-face decisions. It is impossible to forget the image of those SA-men from the early period of Hitler's rule. In them administration and terror found themselves visibly joined; the folder of documents above, and below the high boots. The jargon of authenticity preserves something of this image in words like "commission." In such words there is calculated uncertainty about the distinction between something administratively arranged, justly or unjustly, and something absolutely commanded— between authority and sentiment.

The incorporation of the word "commission" into the jargon might have been inspired by the first of the *Duino Elegies* of Rilke, who was one of the founders of the jargon. For years every ambitious *Privatdozent* viewed it as an obligatory exercise to analyze that first elegy: "All that was commission." [64] The line expresses the vague feeling that an unsayable element of experience wants something from the subject. This is similarly the case with the archaic torso of Apollo: [65] "Many stars expected you to feel them." [66] To that the poem adds the uncommittedness and vainness of such a feeling of command, especially when it expresses the poetic subject: "But did you manage it?" [67] Rilke absolutizes the word "commission" under the shelter of aesthetic appearance and, as the poem advances, limits the claim that his pathos already announces. The jargon needs only to cross out this limitation, with a deft movement, and to take literally the word "commission," which has been absolutized by questionable poetastering. But the fact that the neoromantic lyric sometimes behaves like the jargon, or at least timidly readies the way for it, should not lead us to look for the evil of the poetry simply in its form. It is not simply grounded, as a much too innocent view might maintain, in the mixture of poetry and prose. Both of them become unequally untrue from the same cause. The evil, in the neoromantic lyric, consists in the fitting out of the words with a theological overtone, which is belied by the condition of the lonely and secular subject who is speaking there: religion as ornament. Where words and turns of this

64. Rainer Maria Rilke, *Duineser Elegien* (New York, n.d.), p. 8.
65. Cf. Rainer Maria Rilke, *Der neuen Gedichte anderer Teil* (Leipzig, 1919) p. 1.
66. Rilke, *Duineser Elegien*, p. 7.
67. *Ibid.*, p. 8.

sort appear in Hölderlin—the secret model for all this —they are not yet the tremulous expressions of the jargon, however uninhibitedly the administrators of the jargon reach out their hands toward that unprotected genius. In lyric poetry, as in philosophy, the jargon acquires its defining character by the way it imputes its truth. It does this by making an intended object present—as though this object were Being without any tension toward the subject. That makes it, prior to all discursive judgment, into untruth. The expression is sufficient unto itself. It discards as an annoyance the obligation to express a thing other than itself. Beyond its difference from that thing, which may already be nothing, and out of thanks, this nothing is made into that which is supreme. Rilke's language still stands on the edge of all this, like much that is irrational from the era prior to fascism. It not only darkens, but it also takes note of, subconscious material, which, slipping away from thingly rationality, protests against it. The feeling of being touched, which the word "commission" is supposed to evoke in that elegy, is of such a nature. It at once becomes unbearable as soon as it objectifies itself, as soon as it flaunts itself as something definite and unambiguous precisely in its irrationality. It is unbearable in all its registers; from Heidegger's obedient and comprehending thought to all that summoning and invoking, with whose details the subaltern self-importance of the jargon surrounds itself. Simply because Rilke, in this poem, acknowledges the multiple significance of commission, that multiple significance expects to be absolved. On the other hand, though, commission without committing agent is already used here, as in the jargon; and a conception of Being in general is evoked which fits this usage. That again accords with the handicraftish religiosity of the early Rilke, especially of the *Book of Hours*, which with theological phrasings subjects the psychological to a kind of refining process.

Lyric poetry permits itself any metaphor, even the absolutely unmetaphorical, as a parable. It will not be disturbed by the question of the objectivity of those things that are allegedly suggested to the subject by its emotions. Nor will the lyric be disturbed by the question of whether the words, gathered from culture, at all cover the experiences whose objectification is the central idea of such lyric. Therefore, because it blunts itself against the truth and exactitude of its words—even the vaguest would have to be smuggled in as something vague, not as something definite— this lyric, as lyric, is already bad, despite its virtuosity. The problematic of that to which it claims to elevate itself, the problematic of its content, is also that of its form, which makes believe it could be capable of transcendence, and in that way becomes mere appearance in a more fateful sense than that of the aesthetic.

The evil truth behind that appearance, nonetheless, is precisely the bond between commission and the administrative structure, a bond which denies that appearance in the service of that structure. Its words are dossier numbers, or stamps, or that *In re* of official office language, which it remains the commission of the jargon to gloss over. The fussy attention to individual words, as they were lexically handled in the days of the pre-Heideggerian idol-phenomenology, was already the harbinger of bureaucratic stocktaking. Whoever prepared meanings from all this, whoever acted as a midwife of today's pure words, acted by force, without regard for the sanctuaries of the philosophy of Being. The method which prohibits a word from being involved with its neighbors was, objectively, of the same character as the small bureaucrat, who sees to it that everything remains strictly in its category, as he himself remains in his salary-class. Even death is handled by the book, in SS-orders and in existential philosophies; red tape ridden as Pegasus, ridden in extremis as an apocalyptic steed. In the jargon the sun, which the jargon has in its heart, brings the dark secret of the method to the light of day, as the method of a procedure which eagerly takes the place of the intended object. In general, the jargon behaves in this way itself. Indifferent to the matter at hand, it is to be used for commanded purposes. Language, as once in major philosophy, no longer flows out of the necessity of the subject matter. Such language-procedural indifference has become a metaphysics of language: that which in terms of its form seems to fly above its correlative, thereby establishes itself as something higher. The less philosophical systematizing, which Nietzsche called dishonest, is theoretically possible, the more that which had its place only in the system transforms itself into mere assertion. In effect, linguistic nonsense is the heir of the disintegrated strictness of the system. In fact, like a worthless construction, it is forever falling off its stilts and stumbling around in nonsense.

The term "commission" sets itself up with unquestioned authority in the vulgar jargon of authenticity. The fallibility of the term is hushed up by the absolute use of the word. By leaving out of consideration the organizations and people which give commissions, the term establishes itself as a linguistic eyrie of totalitarian orders. It does this without rational examination of the 'right of those who usurp for themselves the charisma of the leader. Shy theology allies itself with secular brazenness. There exist cross-connections between the jargon of authenticity and old school-like phrases, like that which was once observed by Tucholsky: "That's the way it's done here." The same holds true for the trick of military command, which dresses an imperative in the guise of a predicative sentence. By eliminating all linguistic traces of the will of the superior, that which is intended is given greater emphasis. Thus the impression is created that it is necessary to obey, since what is demanded already occurs factually. "The participants on this trip, in memory of our heroes, assemble in Lüneburg." Heidegger, too, cracks the whip when he italicizes the auxiliary verb in the sentence, "Death *is*." [68] The grammatical translation of the imperative into a predication makes the imperative categorical. This imperative does not allow for refusal, since it no longer at all obliges like the Kantian imperative, but describes obedience as a completed fact. Possible resistance is then eliminated simply in terms of logical form. The objection raised

68. Heidegger, *Being and Time*, p. 303.

by reason is banned from the range of what is at all conceivable in society. Such irrationality, in an element which still, in times of pawned-off myths, insists on calling itself thinking, was, of course, the blemish of the Kantian enlightenment. The Kantian enlightenment asserts deceptively that it is not necessary to know the categorical imperative in order to act rightly. Meanwhile, the categorical imperative, if it is truly to be one with the principles of reason, trusts that each one who acts has reason, which if unimpaired would be philosophical reason.

Christian Schütze has published a satire called the "Stenciled Speech for Festive Occasions." It throws light on the jargon with great comic force:

Most honored Mr. President, ministers, secretaries of state, mayors, advisors, administrators, and assistants, highly esteemed men and women of our cultural life, representatives of science, of industry, and of the self-employed middle-class, honored public of this festive gathering, ladies and gentlemen!

It is not by chance that we are gathered here today for the purpose of celebrating this day. In a time like ours, in which the true human values have more than ever to be our innermost concern, a statement is expected from us. I do not wish to present you with a patented solution, but I would merely like to bring up for discussion a series of hot potatoes which do after all face us. For we do not need ready-made opinions, which anyway do not touch us deeply, but what we need is rather the genuine dialogue which moves us in our humanity. What brought us together here is our knowledge of the power of encounter in the forming of the intrahuman sphere. The things which matter are settled in this intrahuman sphere. I do not have to tell you what I mean by this. You will all understand me, for in a particular and extraordinary sense you all have to do with people.

In a time like ours—I have mentioned it already—in which the perspective of things has everywhere begun to waver, everything depends more than ever on the individual who knows of the essence of things, of things as such, of things in their authenticity. We need openhearted people who are capable of this. Who are these people?—you will ask me—and I will answer you: You are they! By being gathered here you have proven more thoroughly than by words that you are prepared to put emphasis on your concern. That is what I would like to thank you for. But I would also like to thank you for energetically opposing, by your commitment to this good cause, the flood of materialism which threatens to drown everything around us. To say it in a nutshell from the start: you have come here to be given directions; you have come to listen. From this encounter, on an intrahuman level, you expect a contribution to the reestablishment of the interhuman climate. You expect a restoration of that homey warmth which seems to be lacking, in our modern industrial society, to such a terrifying degree. . . .

But what does this mean for our concrete situation here and now? To pronounce the question means to pose it. But in fact it means much more than that. It means that we expose ourselves to it, that we surrender to it. That we must not forget. But in the rush and busy work of the day, modern man forgets it all too easily. But you who belong to the silent majority, you know of it. For our problems stem from a region which it is our vocation to preserve. The wholesome perplexity which comes from this situation opens perspectives which we should not simply block out by turning away in boredom. It is important to think with the heart and to tune in the human antenna to the same wave length. Today no ones knows better than man that which is of importance in the end.[69]

Now, everything is assembled here: the innermost concern, the true dialogue, things in their authenticity, with a vague reminiscence of Heidegger, the encounter on an intrahuman level, the question for its own sake, even the slightly anachronistic reserve army of the silent majority. The long-winded address designates the participating notables in terms of their function and subordinates the whole speech from the beginning to an intangible administrative purpose. While what the speaker is aiming at remains unspecified, the jargon brings it to light. The concern is the working climate. By calling the listeners people "who in a particular and extraordinary sense have to do with people," it can be gathered that the subject matter is that kind of human leadership in which men are merely the pretext for leadership-in-itself. To this is accurately fitted the indestructible phrase about the "flood of materialism" which full-blooded industrial leaders usually vituperate in those who are dependent on them. That is the ground of being of the higher element in the jargon. In its slips of the tongue the jargon acknowledges that administration is its essence. The intrahuman level, which is supposed to contribute to the "reestablishment of the human climate," places the word "level" beside "intrahuman," together with the association of "I and thou," which has a social-scientific as well as a homey character. The levels, how-

69. Christian Schütze, "Gestanzte Festansprache," in *Stuttgarter Zeitung*, Dec. 2, 1962, quoted in *Der Monat*, Jan., 1963, p. 63, n. 160.

ever—the level of counties, of the federation—designate areas of judicial and administrative responsibility. The exhortation to think with the heart—Pascal's formula *que les grandes pensées proviennent du coeur* —has been admired by business men right from the beginning; it is pronounced with the same breath as "the human antenna is tuned in to the same wave length." The total content, however, is flowering nonsense. This becomes obvious in phrases like "To pronounce the question is to pose it," or, "No one knows better than man that which is of importance in the end." Such nonsense also has its reasonable basis in the world. It hides the fact that both *it* and the goal at which it aims are manipulated. For this reason all content is "bracketed," as it goes in administrative German. At the same time the appearance of content must not be renounced; those who are addressed, again in the same German, must "toe the line." The purpose, the intention, contracts itself into an intentionless underworldly language, truthful to the objective determination of the jargon itself, which has no other content than its wrapping.

After the fact, the jargon adapts itself to the need for a philosophy which was current in about 1925. This was a philosophy that strove for the concretization of experience, thought, and behavior in the midst of a total state of affairs which oriented itself according to something abstract—according to exchange. For this reason the jargon is neither able nor willing to concretize the elements which condemn it to abstractness. The jargon turns in a circle. It wants to be immediately concrete without sliding into mere facticity. It is consequently forced into secret abstraction, which is the same formalism against which Heidegger's own school, that of phenomenology, once strongly spoke out. This can be grasped in existential ontology's theoretical criticism, especially in the paired concepts of authenticity and inauthenticity in *Sein und Zeit*. Already there the drive for concretion is coupled with a hands-off attitude. One speaks from a depth which would be profaned if it were called content. Yet this depth wants to be this content, which in turn wants to express itself. Heidegger's defensive technique of withdrawing into eternity takes place at this "pure and disgusting height" of which Hegel spoke in his polemic against Reinhold.[70] Like Reinhold, Heidegger cannot get enough of the ritual preliminaries for the "step into the temple," [71] although hardly anyone nowadays dares to tie a warning bell around the cat's neck. Heidegger is by no means incomprehensible, as one might gather from the marginalia of the positivists, but he lays around himself the taboo that any understanding of him would simultaneously be falsification. The impossibility of saving what this thinking wants to save is cleverly turned into its own life element. This thinking refuses all content which would have to be argued against. Metaphysics is said to miss this element in the same manner as it is missed in translation into ontic statements, which, as parts of the individual

70. G. W. F. Hegel, *Werke,* ed. H. Glockner (Stuttgart, 1958) Vol. I: "Differenz des Fichteschen und Schellingschen Systems," p. 43.
71. *Ibid.*

scientific disciplines, are regarded with some favor.[72] Even authenticity and inauthenticity are first of all treated cautiously. Heidegger shuns the reproach that he paints in black and white. He claims that he does not give a directive for philosophical judgment, but that he introduces descriptive and neutral terms in the manner of that which in earlier phenomenology was called investigation. In Weber's interpretation of sociology, a discipline denounced by Heidegger, this was called neutrality of values:

> As modes of Being, *authenticity* and *inauthenticity* (these expressions have been chosen terminologically in a strict sense) are both grounded in the fact that any Dasein whatsoever is characterized by mineness. But the inauthenticity of Dasein does not signify any "less"

72. Careless for one moment, Heidegger shows his hand in the tractatus on *Identität und Differenz:*

But let us assume for a moment that difference is an element added by our representation. Then the question rises: added to what? The answer is, to the existent. All right. But what does this mean—the existent? What else does it mean but such a thing as is? Thus we enter the supposed addition, the conception of difference under being. But "Being" says itself: being which is existent? Where we wanted to take difference as supposed addition we already always find what is existent and being in their difference. It is the same story as Grimm's fairy tale about the hare and the hedgehog: "I'm here already." (Heidegger, *Identität und Differenz* [Pfüllingen, 1957], p. 60.)

What is said here about so-called ontological difference by means of a rather primitive hypostasis of the copula, is said in order to shift the ontological primacy of difference into being itself. This is actually Heidegger's method. This method protects itself by considering possible contradictions as elements that have already been considered in the particular thesis. These are false syllogisms which any logician could check. These false syllogisms are projected into, and thus justified by, the objective structure of that at which the thought aims.

94

Being or any "lower" degree of Being. Rather it is the case that even in its fullest concretion Dasein can be characterized by inauthenticity—when busy, when excited, when interested, when ready for enjoyment.[73]

In a much later passage of *Sein und Zeit,* the category of "the They" is subsumed under inauthenticity. In this passage Heidegger says

that interpretation is purely ontological in its aims, and is far removed from any moralizing critique of everyday Dasein, and from the aspirations of a "philosophy of culture." . . . Even the expression "idle talk" is not to be used here in a "disparaging" signification.[74]

The quotation marks around "disparaging" are the kid gloves of a prudish metaphysics. Considerable advantages are connected with this kind of methodological performance. The affirmations of scientific purity in Husserl's texts provide the model for all this. The philosophy of authenticity needs its proviso clauses so that it can on occasion make the excuse that it is not a philosophy. The reputation of scientific objectivity grows together with its authority and, at the same time, leaves the decision between authentic and inauthentic being up to an arbitrariness—one that has been absolved from the judgment of reason, in a fashion not much different from Max Weber's "value." The execution of the volte is so elegant because "the terminologically chosen" expressions are not exhausted by the uses of them that are chosen in subjective freedom. Rather, and Heidegger the philosopher of language should be the first to concede this, they keep as

73. Heidegger, *Being and Time,* p. 68.
74. *Ibid.,* p. 211.

their objective content those standards from which Heidegger distinguishes them. The nominalists saw that better than the latecomer of language mysticism. Following Bacon's doctrine of idols, Hobbes already noted "that men usually express their affects simultaneously with words so that the latter already include a certain judgment on the subject matter." [75] The triviality of this observation does not free us from the responsibility of reminding people of it when they merely ignore it. As an impartial contemplative of essence, Heidegger allows for the fact that inauthenticity "can define existence in its fullest concretion." Yet the accompanying words, which he attributes to this mode of being, are essentially vituperative. As officiousness and interestedness, they characterize such qualities as have given themselves up to the world of exchange and wares and resemble this world. Somebody is officious when he carries on business activity for his own sake and confuses means with ends. If a person is "interested," it means that—all too openly according to the rules of the bourgeois game—he sees to his own interest, or disguises as his objective that which only serves himself. Pleasure capacity falls in the same line. According to the habit of the *petit bourgeois*, the deformations inflicted on men by the world of profit are explained by men's greed, as if it was their fault that they were cheated out of their subjectivity. In the end, however, Heidegger's philosophy does not want to have anything to do with the cultural

75. Quoted in Rudolf Eucken, *Geschichte der philosophischen Terminologie* (Leipzig, 1879), p. 86, in reference to Thomas Hobbes, *Leviathan,* chaps. 4 and 5.

philosophy in which such questions appear. And indeed, the concept of cultural philosophy is just as ridiculous as that of social philosophy. The limitation of philosophy to one specific area is incompatible with the fact that it should reflect on institutional separation. For philosophy should itself derive this separation, and recognize that which is necessarily separated as something which then again is not separated. By virtue of its self-limitation, cultural philosophy accepts the division of phenomena into areas of subject matter and possibly even into those of hierarchy within areas. In the structure of alleged levels the place of culture is almost unavoidably a derived one. For this reason a philosophy which enjoys itself fastidiously in this sphere would be satisfied with that which officials patronize as essayism. By the same token it would avoid that which has been handed down under the name of constitutive problems, which, of course, could only be stubbornly ignored by such a philosophy. Heidegger keeps that in mind. He is familiar, on the one hand, with Husserl's schema of philosophical-eidetic disciplines, and, on the other, of disciplines which are directed toward objects—both of which disciplines he melted together with the idealistic criticism of reification. But an overtone of the word "cultural-philosophical" cannot fail to be heard in Heidegger. He defames that which sticks like a parasite to what is secondary, to life which has already been produced. He acts peevish toward any form of mediation, even in the mind which is itself essentially mediation. The growth climate of this hostility to cultural philosophy is that academic climate in which they admonished the Jew

Georg Simmel, on the grounds that, at least in intention, he absorbed himself in that concretion which the systems were forever only promising. Thus he transgressed a taboo of traditional philosophy which busies itself, if not with the fundamental themes of occidental metaphysics, at least with the question of their possibility. Criticism of the limitations of cultural philosophy is vengefully limited. The chemically pure concept of philosophy, as the inquiry into an unruined essence, underneath that which has only been made and posited by men, is worth just as little as that limited cultural philosophy. The subject area of the pure has no advantage over culture, whether this pure essence be considered as a truthfully philosophical element, as something merely explanatory, or as a supporting element. It is, rather, like culture, a determination of reflection. While specialistic cultural philosophy absolutizes the form of that which has become, against that on which it feeds, fundamental ontology embezzles its own cultural mediation, insofar as it shies away from a spirit which is concretized in objectivity. Whatever the possibilities of natural philosophy may be nowadays, primalness now has the same place in the philosophical atlas in which nature was once registered. This primalness is as much a part, as not, of that which fundamental ontology despises as culture. Culture includes even the material infrastructure of society, in which human work and thought are rooted, and the only means by which work becomes real societal work. This does not mean that the contrast to the suprastructure becomes any less sharp. Philosophical nature has to be regarded as history, and history as nature. The contrast between primal experiences and cultural experiences, which Gundolf invented *ad hoc* for George, was ideology in the midst of the suprastructure, devised for the purpose of obscuring the contrast between infrastructure and ideology. The categories which he popularized, and among which even the later, more successful, category of godlike being is present, were marketed as substantial;[76] while precisely in neoromanticism cultural mediation stands out blatantly, in the form of the *Jugendstil*. Bloch rightfully made fun of Gundolf for his belief in today's primal experiences. These primal experiences were a warmed-over piece of expressionism. They were later made into a permanent institution by Heidegger, under the benediction of public opinion. What he dislikes in dealing with culture, to which, incidentally, his own philological divagations belong, is the business of starting with the experience of something derived. But this cannot be avoided and has to be taken into consciousness. In the universally mediated world everything experienced in primary terms is culturally preformed. Whoever wants the other has to start with the immanence of culture, in order to break out through it. But fundamental ontology gladly spares itself that, by pretending it has a starting point somewhere outside. In that way such ontology succumbs to cultural mediations all the more; they recur as social aspects of that ontology's own purity. Philosophy involves itself all the

76. Cf. Friedrich Gundolf, *George,* 3d ed. (Berlin, 1930) p. 269.

more deeply in society as it more eagerly—reflecting upon itself—pushes off from society and its objective spirit. It claws itself firmly into its blindly social fate, which—in Heidegger's terminology—has thrown one into this and no other place. That was according to the taste of fascism. With the downfall of market liberalism, relationships of domination stepped nakedly into the foreground. The baldness of their order, the authentic law of the "needy time," easily permits itself to be taken for something primal. That is how people could jaw about blood and soil, without a smile, during the excessively accumulating industrial capitalism of the Third Reich. The jargon of authenticity continues all that, less tangibly—with impunity, because at that time social differences occasionally led to conflicts —such as those between the primary-school teacher appointed to ordinarius and the career professor, or between the official optimism of the deadly war machine and the philosophical frowning of far too autocratic enthusiasts, who were deeply attracted to Being unto death.

Heidegger's complaints against cultural philosophy have fateful consequences in the ontology of authenticity: what this ontology at first bans into the sphere of cultural mediation it now shoves directly on into hell. To be sure, the world is similar enough to hell, dipped as the world is in a gloomy flood of nonsense, the fallen form of language. Karl Kraus compressed that fact into the thesis that today the phrase gives birth to reality—especially to that reality which arose, after the catastrophe, under the name of culture. To a great extent that reality is, as Valéry defined politics, only there to keep men away from what is of importance to them. In agreement with Kraus, whom he does not mention, Heidegger says in *Sein und Zeit:*

> Hearing and understanding have attached themselves beforehand to what is said-in-the-talk as such." [77]

So the business of communication and its formulas cut in between the matter and the subject, and blind the subject against precisely that which all the chatter is about. "What is said-in-the-talk as such spreads in wider circles and takes on an authoritative character. Things are so because one says so." [78] But Heidegger imposes the critical diagnosis of a negative ontological presence on the "everyday being of the *Da,* existence," which in truth is historical in nature: the entangling of the mind with the sphere of circulation, at a stage in which the objective spirit is covered by the economic utilization process, as if by a fungus which stifles the quality of thought. This confusion has arisen and can be gotten rid of; we do not need to bemoan it and leave it in peace as if it were the essence of Dasein. Heidegger rightly perceives the abstractness of chatter "as such," which has emptied itself of any relationship to its content; but from the aberrant abstractness of chatter he draws conclusions as to its metaphysical invariance, however questionable that may be. Chatter would already be in decline if, in a reasonable economy, the expenditure of advertisements disappeared. Chatter is forced on men by a social structure which

77. Heidegger, *Being and Time,* p. 212.
78. *Ibid.*

negates them as subjects long before this is done by the newspaper companies. But Heidegger's critique becomes ideological by grasping the emancipated spirit as that which becomes of it under supremely real engagements, and by doing so without making distinctions. He condemns idle chatter, but not brutality, the alliance with which is the true guilt of chatter, which is in itself far more innocent. As soon as Heidegger wants to silence chatter, his language clatters with weaponry:

> To be able to keep silent, Dasein must have something to say—that is, it must have at its disposal an authentic and rich disclosedness of itself. In that case one's reticence . . . makes something manifest, and does away with "idle talk." [79]

His language itself speaks forth, as seldom elsewhere, from the word "to strike down"; it is a language of power. But it has already been seen in the Hitlerian realm that the goal of this language is at one with the state of affairs which it indicts. Heidegger believes that under the domination of the *They* nobody needs to take responsibility for anything:

> The "they" is there alongside everywhere, . . . but in such a manner that it has always stolen away whenever Dasein presses for a decision. Yet because the "they" presents every judgment and decision as its own, it deprives the particular Dasein of its answerability. The "they" can, as it were, manage to have "them" constantly invoking it. It can be answerable for everything most easily, because it is not someone who needs to vouch for anything. It "was" always the "they" who

79. *Ibid.*, p. 208.

did it, and yet it can be said that it has been "no one."
In Dasein's everydayness the agency through which
most things come about is one of which we must say
that "it was no one." [80]

That is precisely what came to pass under National
Socialism, as the universal *Befehlsnotstand*,[81] that
state of emergency which torturers later use as their
excuse. Heidegger's sketch of the They comes closest
to what it is, the exchange relationship, when he is
treating averageness:

> The "they" has its own ways in which to be. That
> tendency of Being-with which we have called "distan-
> tiality" is grounded in the fact that Being-with-one-
> another concerns itself as such with *averageness,*
> which is an existential characteristic of the "they." The
> "they," in its Being, essentially makes an issue of this.
> Thus the "they" maintains itself factically in the aver-
> ageness of that which belongs to it, of that which it re-
> gards as valid and that which it does not, and of that to
> which it grants success and that to which it denies it. In
> this averageness with which it prescribes what can and
> may be ventured, it keeps watch over everything excep-
> tional that thrusts itself to the fore. Every kind of pri-
> ority gets noiselessly suppressed. Overnight, everything
> that is primordial gets glossed over as something that
> has long been well known. Everything gained by a strug-
> gle becomes just something to be manipulated. Every
> secret loses its force. This care of averageness reveals in
> turn an essential tendency of Dasein which we call the
> "levelling" down . . . of all possibilities of Being." [82]

80. *Ibid.*, p. 165.
81. [*Befehlsnotstand:* morally compelling situation for a
soldier, who must carry out an order with which he cannot
square his conscience.]
82. Heidegger, *Being and Time*, pp. 164–65.

That leveling is described as violence, in the manner of elites which claim that "prerogative" for themselves. It is a leveling which they themselves want to employ, and is no other than the leveling which occasionally befalls the exchanger, through his inevitable reduction to the equivalence form; the critique of political economy grasping exchange value in terms of the social work-time which on the average has to be spent. In its hostility to the negatively ontologized They, the opposition to capitalist anonymity eagerly overlooks the law of value which is asserting itself—a suffering which will not have it said what it is suffering from. When that anonymity, whose social source is unmistakable, is analyzed as a possibility of being, then that society is exonerated which simultaneously both disqualifies and determines the relationships of its members.

The mobility of words unquestionably continued their degradation from the beginning. In the functional word, deception is posited simultaneously with the exchange principle itself and grasps spirit; because this latter cannot be without the idea of truth, it exhibits flagrantly what has entrenched itself in material praxis behind the free and upright exchange of goods. But without mobility language would never have become capable of that relation to the matter at hand, by whose criterion Heidegger judges communicative language. Language philosophy, in the question of communicative language, would have to investigate the metamorphosis of quantity into the quality of mere chatter, or, better, the interinvolvement of both aspects; and would not proceed in an authoritarian spirit to sort out the wheat from the chaff of language. No thinking could unfold itself into the not-yet-thought without that shot of irresponsibility over which Heidegger grows so excited; in that, the spoken distinguishes itself from the authentically written word, and even in the latter positivists can easily criticize as irresponsible that which goes beyond what is the case. Immaturity and timidity stand no higher than chatter. Even that linguistic objectivity which presupposes the utmost alertness toward the phrase also has as its precondition mobility of expression, no matter how broken: urbanity. Nobody can write without phrases, and who is true to the matter who is not also a literate person? The defense of this kind of person seems to be in place after the murder of the Jews. Kraus himself despised the illiterate, if possible even more than the literate. On the other hand the summary judgment concerning idle talk, which insinuates it through a negative ontology, constantly permits the justification of the phrase as if it were fate. Once idle talk is a state of mind, one need not be greatly embarrassed when authenticity turns into idle talk. That is happening today to Heidegger's own legend. We might pull some sentences out of a piece on *The Idea of the German University and the Reform of the German Universities* by Ernst Anrich:

> It is no encroachment [that is, on academic autonomy] when from this Hippocratic oath we make a certain demand, out of our clear knowledge that no specific philosophy can today be placed decisively at the center of the university, a demand that we shall keep alert our universality and our responsiveness in face of the whole of reality; it is no encroachment on this situation when we ask each scholar in this body to carry on his

scholarship under the sign of the final question about
the ground of Being and the whole of Being; and when
we ask him to discuss and exchange these problems
within the whole body, the dignity of which resides
therein. If it is right to demand of the student that the
essence of his study must be to drive forward, within his
own specialty, to the view of Being, and to responsibility
in face of the totality of Being; if that is right, then we
must require of the professor that it be made clear,
through his courses, how his own research is itself
ultimately motivated by a struggle with these questions;
and it may be expected that each of his courses should
be an invoking and awakening force, in this sense.[83]

In an organizational, uncommonly ontic context such
sentences use the jargon of authenticity in just the
way in which Heidegger portrays it in *Sein und Zeit:*
as a characteristic feature of idle talk. The authority
to which in that way the jargon obliges itself is no
other than the authority of the Heideggerian philosophy itself. That in the relevant chapter the author
constantly and rhetorically repeats, "It is no encroach-
ment," is meant to hide precisely such an encroach-
ment; namely, the oath—Anrich himself uses the
mythical word—on the so-called question of Being.
Yet in the same breath the author concedes that no
definite philosophy could today be placed at the center
of the university. It is as though the ominous question
of Being were beyond criticism. Whoever justly spurns
the question of Being together with the chatter about
it had best be sent away entirely. Anrich skillfully

83. Ernst Anrich, *Die Idee der deutschen Universität und
die Reform der deutschen Universitäten,* (Darmstadt, 1960),
p. 114.

latches onto the fact that, in formulas like that of the question concerning the ground of Being, the innocent still hear the sound of resistance against the dispirited atmosphere in which the humanities are today carried on. A human right of students, their need for the essential, becomes blurred in the jargon, in the Heideggerian essence-mythology of Being. The spirit which they miss in the universities is silently converted into the monopoly of an instructional system which, for its part, cried heresy against the spirit when it appeared in the form of reason.

As in the concept of idle chatter, so in that of readiness to hand, which is portrayed with sympathy, and which is the philosophical ancestress of shelteredness, suffering experience is interpreted into its opposite. At some historical stages of agriculture, and in simple wares-economy, production was not radically subordinated to exchange and was nearer to the workers and consumers; and their relationships to one another were not totally reified. The idea of something undisfigured, undeformed, an idea which has yet to be actualized, could hardly have been created without a memory trace of such earlier conditions; although over long periods they probably caused more immediate suffering to those exposed to such conditions than did capitalism. Nonetheless, identifying thought, schooled in exchange, brought the differentiated down to the identity of the concept, and chopped up this more innocent identity. What Hegel and Marx in their youth condemned as alienation and reification, and against which all are spontaneously united today, is what Heidegger interprets ontologically as well as unhistorically, and, in its function as a being-form of Dasein, as something bodily. The ideology of readiness to hand, and its counterpart, strips itself bare in the practice of those devotees of the musical youth movement, who swear to it that a proper fiddle is one that a fiddler has rigged up for himself. Since the artisan forms of production have been overtaken by technology, and are superfluous, the intimacy which adhered to them has become as worthless as the do-it-yourself movement. The unfunctional self-being of things, their freedom from the compulsion of identity, which the dominating mind imposes, would be utopia. It presupposes the alteration of the whole. Nonetheless, in the midst of our all-embracing function context every ontological light on the remains of so-called readiness to hand gilds that context. For its sake the jargon of authenticity speaks as though it were the voice of men and things that are there for their own sake. Through this manoeuver, the jargon becomes all the more a for-others, something for planned and pedagogically decorated effect-contexts. Indeed, the Wagnerian "To be German means to do something for its own sake" accelerated, in slogan form, the export of the German spirit. That spirit competed successfully with the more advanced commodity-thinking of the West, through the slogan's imprimatur, which declared that it was no commodity. That throws light on the artsy-craftsy element in the jargon. It provides a refuge for the stale notion that art should be brought back into life, and that there should be more than art but also more than mere usage. The jargon pursues artisanship under the shadow of industry, as carefully chosen as it is cheap;

it gathers reproductions of kitschy life-reforming impulses that real life has buried under itself, and spares them the hopeless testing ground of actualization. Instead, language rolls up its sleeves and lets it be understood that right action, in the right place, is worth more than reflection. In that way a contemplative attitude, without any perception of the praxis which brings about changes, sympathizes all the more strikingly with the here and now, the servicing of obligations presented within the given.

Heidegger sees himself forced, in the analysis of curiosity, to intimate something of the historical dynamic that necessarily dissolves static relationships.[84] On those relationships the theory of readiness to hand nourishes itself; he leaves it to the gang to call these hale. He sanctions, as an ontological possibility, that "dis-stancing" which is hallowed by its hyphen; that possibility that men might raise themselves above the mere immediacy of the reproduction of their own lives. Nevertheless, he slides into the defaming of consciousness, which has been released from imprisonment:

> Care becomes concern with the possibilities of the seeing the "world" merely as it *looks* while one tarries and takes a rest. Dasein seeks what is far away simply in order to bring it close to itself in the way it looks. Dasein lets itself be carried along . . . solely by the looks of the world; in this kind of Being, it concerns itself with becoming rid of itself as Being-in-the-world and rid of its Being alongside that which, in the closest everyday manner, is ready-to-hand.

84. Heidegger, *Being and Time*, p. 216.

When curiosity has become free, however, it concerns itself with seeing, not in order to understand what
is seen (that is, to come into a Being towards it) but
just in order to see. It seeks novelty only in order to leap
from it anew to another novelty.[85]

For Heidegger, the way to free consciousness is preestablished, inevitable; but it is as little charming to
the man who is freed as are those who are narrowed
by their circle of duties, those who distrust, as artful
and shifty, the mind that is emancipated from praxis.
He equates emancipated consciousness with curiosity.
His hatred toward curiosity is allied to his hatred toward mobility; both are even hammered into the mind
by the ripe old saying: stay in the country and earn
your living honestly. Genetic psychoanalysis knows
the castration threat against the child's sexual investigation; the allegedly suprapsychological stance of the
ontologist fits with the brutal "that's none of your
business," invoked in the castration threat. In the question of curiosity the thinker abuses thinking; without
curiosity the subject would remain imprisoned in a
dull repetition-compulsion and would never open himself up to experience. Of course such an enlightenment
insight is not the whole story. It is equally untrue that,
through Heidegger's admonitions about "the They," that
social state of affairs whose symptoms he reprimands
grows better. It is only that his objection to curiosity
stems from yea-saying at any price:

curiosity has nothing to do with observing entities and
with marvelling at them—θαυμάζειν. To be amazed to

85. *Ibid.*

the point of not understanding is something in which it has no interest. Rather it concerns itself with a kind of knowing, but just in order to have known.[86]

In his *Differenz* essay Hegel criticized curiosity much more searchingly; not as a state of mind but as the position of the reified consciousness with regard to the dead object:

> The living spirit which dwells in a philosophy requires, in order to be released, that it should be brought to birth by a related spirit. It passes by, as an alien phenomenon, any historical conduct which from some kind of interest marches forth to an understanding of opinions; and it does not reveal its interior. To the living spirit it can seem indifferent that it must serve to enlarge the remaining collection of mummies and the general heaps of accidentalia; for it itself has flowed away through the hands curious to collect new pieces of knowledge.[87]

The disagreeable aspect of curiosity, as of greedy nature as a whole, cannot be glossed over. But it is not a probing agitation; rather it is something that reactively, under the pressure of early childhood denial, has emerged from that denial; and which distorts that which once wanted to get free from the always-same, the identical. Curious people are characters whose childish longing for the truth about the sexual was never satisfied; their longing is a shabby substitute. The person from whom that which concerns him was

86. *Ibid.*
87. G. W. F. Hegel, *Werke*, ed. H. Glockner (Stuttgart, 1958), Vol. I: *Aufsätze aus dem Kritischen Journal der Philosophie und andere Aufsätze aus der Jenenser Zeit (Differenzschrift)*, p. 40.

withheld mixes himself evilly into what does not concern him. He becomes enviously enraptured with information over matters in which he himself should not play any part. That is the relation of all greediness to free desire. To Heidegger's arrogance toward the merely ontic, the genesis of curiosity is indifferent. He chalks up mutilation to the fault of the mutilated, as a fault of existence in general. His existential security becomes a heteronomously conditioned activity that is untried by curiosity—idle knowledge. This is probably the original philosophical history of the cliché of commitment. By denouncing a purely ontological possibility according to his own teaching, Heidegger becomes the advocate of the unfullfilment of life. Like the empty phrase of idealism, authenticity, in projecting its existentialism right from the beginning, sides with want, over and against satisfaction and abundance. In spite of its eager neutrality and distance from society, authenticity thus stands on the side of the conditions of production, which, contrary to reason, perpetuate want. When Heidegger finally calls "homelessness" the "third essential characteristic of this phenomenon," [88] he conjures up the Ahasuerian element. He does this by means of the demagogically proven technique of allusion, which keeps quiet about that to which it expects secret consent. The pleasure of mobility becomes a curse for the homeless. The opposite of "everyday Dasein," which "is constantly uprooting itself," [89] is "observing entities and marvelling

88. Heidegger, *Being and Time*, p. 217.
89. *Ibid.*

I I 2

at them," [90] though it is not yet, by any means the contemplation of Being. In philosophy 1927 the rootless intellectual carries the yellow mark of someone who undermines the established order.

How deeply rooted are the societal elements in Heidegger's analysis of authenticity is involuntarily revealed by his use of language. As is well known, Heidegger supplants the traditional category of subjectivity by Dasein, whose essence is existence. Being, however, which "is an *issue* for this entity in its very Being, is in each case mine." [91] This is meant to distinguish subjectivity from all other existent being. It intends, furthermore, to prohibit existence from being "taken ontologically as an instance or special case of some genus of entities as things that are present-at-hand." [92] This construction, which is inspired by Kierkegaard's doctrine of the "transparency" of the self,[93] would like to make possible a starting out from some element of being. This latter is valued as the immediate givenness of the facts of consciousness in traditional epistemology; yet, at the same time, this element of being is supposed to be more than mere fact, in the same manner as the ego of speculative idealism once was. Behind the apersonal "is concerned," nothing more is hidden than the fact that Dasein is consciousness. The entrance of this formula is Heidegger's *scene*

90. *Ibid.,* p. 216.
91. *Ibid.,* p. 67.
92. *Ibid.*
93. Cf. Søren Kierkegaard, *Die Krankheit zum Tode* (Dusseldorf, 1954) p. 10. [English translation by W. Lowrie, *Fear and Trembling, and The Sickness unto Death* (Garden City, N. Y., 1954).]

à faire. From an abstract concept Being turns into something absolute and primary, which is not merely posited. The reason for this lies in the fact that Heidegger reveals an element of Being and calls it Dasein, which would be not just some element of Being, but the pure condition of Being—all this without losing any of the characteristics of individuation, fullness, bodiliness. This is the scheme that the jargon follows, intentionally or unintentionally, to the point of nausea. The jargon cures Dasein from the wound of meaninglessness and summons salvation from the world of ideas into Dasein. Heidegger lays this down once and for all in the title deed, which declares that the person owns himself. The fact that Dasein belongs to itself, that it is "in each case mine," is picked out from individuation as the only general definition that is left over after the dismantling of the transcendental subject and its metaphysics. The *principium individuationis* stands as a principle over and against any particular individual element. At the same time it is that essence. In the case of the former element, the Hegelian dialectical unity of the general and the particular is turned into a relation of possession. Then it is given the rank and rights of the philosophical apriori. "Because Dasein has *in each case mineness* . . . one must always use a *personal* pronoun when one addresses it." [94] The distinction between authenticity and inauthenticity—the real Kierkegaardian one —depends on whether or not this element of being, Dasein, chooses itself, its mineness.[95] Until further

94. Heidegger, *Being and Time*, p. 68.
95. Cf. *Ibid.*

notice, authenticity and inauthenticity have as their criterion the decision in which the individual subject chooses itself as its own possession. The subject, the concept of which was once created in contrast to reification, thus becomes reified. Yet at the same time reification is scoffed at objectively in a form of language which simultaneously commits the same crime. The general concept of mineness, in which this language institutes subjectivity as a possession of itself, sounds like a variant of meanness in Berlin slang. Whatever formerly went under the name of existential and *existentiell* now insists on this new title deed of possession. By the fact that it is ontological, the alternative of authenticity and inauthenticity directs itself according to whether someone decides for himself or not. It takes its directive, beyond real states of affairs, from the highly formal sense of belonging to oneself. Yet its consequences in reality are extremely grave. Once such an ontology of what is most ontic has been achieved, philosophy no longer has to bother about the societal and natural-historical origin of this title deed, which declares that the individual owns himself. Such a philosophy need no longer be concerned with how far society and psychology allow a man to be himself or become himself, or whether in the concept of such selfness the old evil is concentrated one more time. The societal relation, which seals itself off in the identity of the subject, is de-societalized into an in-itself. The individual, who himself can no longer rely on any firm possession, holds on to himself in his extreme abstractness as the last, the supposedly unlosable possession. Metaphysics ends in a miserable consolation: after all, one still remains what one is. Since men do not remain what they are by any means, neither socially nor biologically, they gratify themselves with the stale remainder of self-identity as something which gives distinction, both in regard to being and meaning. This unlosable element, which has no substratum but its own concept, the tautological selfness of the self, is to provide the ground, as Heidegger calls it, which the authentics possess and the inauthentics lack. The essence of Dasein, i.e., what is more than its mere existence, is nothing but its selfness: it is itself. The quarrel with Heidegger's language is not the fact that it is permeated, like any philosophical language, with figures from an empirical reality which it would like to transcend, but that it transforms a bad empirical reality into transcendence.

Heidegger is careful to have alibis against the charge of epistemological subjectivism. Mineness, or the self-sameness of the authentically existing self, is to be separated from the identity of the subject.[96] Otherwise, these would break through the idealism of a thinking that claims to be a thinking of origins. But Heidegger's Being, to which, after all, some considerable creative acts are attributed, becomes the Fichtean absolute ego. It appears beheaded, as it were, in contrast to the traditional, merely posited ego. But the distinction from Fichte does not hold. If the distinguishing element, the fact that mineness belongs to real persons, was not their abstractly preordained principle, their ontological primacy would be done for.

96. *Ibid.*, p. 168.

Meanwhile, even the old-fashioned idealist identity depended on elements of fact as conditions of its own possibility, insofar as it was precisely the unity of the representations of a consciousness. Almost unrecognizably, all this rises again in Heidegger's thought, in a reinterpretation that turns it into the hinge of his whole argument. Heidegger's point of departure turns against possible criticism, in the same manner as Hegel's once turned against the philosophy of reflection. Criticism is said to miss a newly discovered or rediscovered structure, beyond the dualism of fact and essence, which was still taught by Husserl in traditional fashion. Not only Heidegger's philosophy, but also the whole jargon of authenticity that follows, depends on the staging of the elaboration of this structure. It is pointed out at a very early stage in *Sein und Zeit,* where Heidegger deals with the primacy of Dasein. Heidegger interprets subjectivity as a concept of indifference: essence and fact in one. The primacy of Dasein is said to be twofold. On the one hand it is to be ontic, namely, determined by existence. In other words, existence defines something in the nature of fact, something existent. On the other hand "Dasein is in itself 'ontological,' because existence is thus determinative for it." [97] Thus something contradictory to subjectivity is immediately attributed to subjectivity: that it be itself fact and reality, and, in line with the demand of traditional philosophy, that as consciousness it make facticity possible. As the latter it becomes pure concept, in contrast to facticity; it becomes es-

97. *Ibid.,* p. 34.

sence and finally Husserl's *eidos ego*. Against the traditional doctrine of the subject this double character, which is also an absolute unity before the fall into differentiation, claims the rank of an important discovery. For that reason Heidegger uses an archaizing, scholastic method. Both these characteristics of the subject he ascribes to Dasein, as attributes, without considering that they conflict with the principle of contradiction when they are attached in this way. According to Heidegger, Dasein "is" not merely ontic, which would be tautological in regard to what is grasped under the concept of Dasein, but it is also ontological. In this predication of the ontic and the ontological, from the standpoint of Dasein, the falsity of the regressive element can be recognized. The concept of the ontological cannot be attached to a substratum, as if ontological were its predicate. To be a fact is no predicate which can attach itself to a concept; and, since Kant's criticism of the ontological proof of the existence of God, any philosophy should be careful not to affirm this. The same holds true for the nonfacticity of concepts, their essentiality. This essentiality is localized in the relation of the concept to the facticity that is synthesized in it—and never belongs to it, as Heidegger suggests, as a quality of it itself. To say that Dasein "is ontic or ontological," can, strictly speaking, not be judged at all, for what is meant by existence is a substratum. It is for this reason that the meaning of Dasein is nonconceptual. In contrast to this, "ontic" and "ontological" are expressions for different forms of reflection, and are thus unable only in regard to the definitions of Dasein, or to the position of such definitions in theory—not immediately, however, in regard to the meant substratum itself. Their place is that of conceptual mediation. Heidegger declares this to be immediacy *sui generis*. Dasein thus suddenly becomes a third element, without regard to the fact that the dual character that Heidegger bends together into this third can by no means be regarded independently from that which happens conceptually to the substratum. In Heidegger, the fact that there is nothing which maintains itself identically without the categorical unity, and the fact that this categorical unity does not maintain itself without that which it synthesizes—such facts take the form of the elements which are to be distinguished. These elements in turn take the form of derivatives. There is nothing between heaven and earth that is in itself ontic or ontological; rather, everything becomes what it is only by means of the constellation into which it is brought by philosophy. Language had a means for making this differentiation when it spoke of ontological theories, judgments, and proofs instead of something ontological *sans façon*. By means of an objectification of this kind, such an element would of course already be turned into that ontic against which the literal meaning of "ontological" sharpens itself: the logos of something ontic. After *Sein und Zeit* Heidegger tried to interpret the *Critique of Pure Reason* in terms of his project. Yet previously, he had done something very similar to what Kant criticized in the rationalistic form of ontology: an amphiboly of the concepts of reflection. Heidegger may have missed the mistake, but it is to the advantage of his project. According to usual terminology, it is obvious that the concept that says what essentially belongs to something that is, is ontological. If, however, this becomes unnoticeably the ontological essence of the existent in itself, then the result is a concept of Being that is prior to the concepts of reflection. At first this occurs in *Sein und Zeit* through the hypostasis of an ontological sphere that is the nourishment for all of Heidegger's philosophy. The amphiboly resides in the following: in the concept of the subject two elements flow together—the subject's own definition as something existent, in which form it still remains fixed in the Kantian interlocking of the transcendental subject with the unity of consciousness per se, and, secondly, the definition of subject as constituent of everything existent. This togetherness is unavoidable in the concept of subject. It is an expression of the dialectic between subject and object in the subject itself, and evidence of its own conceptuality. Without mediation subjectivity cannot be brought to either of its extremes, which belong to different *genera*. This aforementioned unavoidability becomes an imaginary thing by virtue of the deficiency of the concept: mediation toward the immediate identity of the mediating and mediated elements. Certainly one element is not without the other, but the two are by no means one, as Heidegger's fundamental thesis alleges. In their identity, identity thinking would have swallowed up the nonidentical element, the existent, which the word Dasein intends. Thus Heidegger secretly reinstates the creator quality of the absolute subject, which was supposedly avoided, as it were, by starting with mineness in each case. The notion of the double character of Dasein, as ontic and ontological, expels Dasein from itself. This is Heidegger's disguised idealism. For the dialectic in the subject between the existent and the concept becomes being of a higher order; and the dialectic is brought to a halt. Whatever praises itself for reaching behind the concepts of reflection—subject and object—in order to grasp something substantial, does nothing but reify the irresolvability of the concepts of reflection. It reifies the impossibility of reducing one into the other, into the in-itself. This is the standard philosophical form of underhanded activity, which thereupon occurs constantly in the jargon. It vindicates without authority and without theology, maintaining that what is of essence is real, and, by the same token, that the existent is essential, meaningful, and justified.

In spite of Heidegger's assertion, mineness, and consequently authenticity, result in pure identity. How true this is can be shown *e contrario*. Whatever is inauthentic for him, all the categories of the They are those in which a subject is not itself, is unidentical with itself. Thus for example the category of *Unverweilen,* as a giving oneself over to the world;[98] the subject gives itself up to something other, instead of remaining with itself and "being knowingly in the truth." [99] What was a necessary element in the experience of consciousness, in Hegelian phenomenology, becomes anathema for Heidegger, since he compresses the experience of consciousness into self-experience. However, identity, the hollow kernel of such selfness,

98. *Ibid.,* p. 216.
99. *Ibid.*

thus takes the place of idea. Even the cult of selfness is reactionary. The concept of selfness is here being eternalized precisely at the moment in which it has already disintegrated. Late bourgeois thinking re-forms itself into naked self-preservation, into the early bourgeois principle of Spinoza: *sese conservare*. But whoever stubbornly insists on his mere so-being, because everything else has been cut off from him, only turns his so-being into a fetish. Cut off and fixed selfness only becomes, all the more, something external. This is the ideological answer to the fact that the current state of affairs is everywhere producing an ego weakness which eradicates the concept of subject as individuality. That weakness as well as its opposite march into Heidegger's philosophy. Authenticity is supposed to calm the consciousness of weakness, but it also resembles it. By it the living subject is robbed of all definition, in the same way as it loses its attributes in reality. However, what is done to men by the world becomes the ontological possibility of the inauthenticity of men. From that point it is only a step to the usual criticism of culture, which self-righteously picks on shallowness, superficiality, and the growth of mass culture.

The preterminological use of "authentic" underlined what was essential to a thing, in contrast to what was accidental. Whoever is dissatisfied with silly examples from textbooks needs to deliberate by himself; this will help more than a developed theory to assure him of what is essential. What is essential in phenomena, and what is accidental, hardly ever springs straightforwardly out of the phenomena. In order to be determined in its objectivity, it has first to be reflected on subjectively. Certainly, at first glance, it seems more essential to a worker that he has to sell his working power, that the means of production do not belong to him, that he produces material goods, than that he is a member of a suburban gardening club; although the worker himself may think that the latter is more essential. However, as soon as the question directs itself to so central a concept as capitalism, Marx and the verbal definitions of Max Weber say something extremely different from each other. In many cases the distinction between essential and inessential, between authentic and inauthentic, lies with the arbitrariness of definition, without in the least implying the relativity of truth. The reason for this situation lies in language. Language uses the term "authentic" in a floating manner. The word also wavers according to its weightiness, in the same way as occasional expressions. The interest in the authenticity of a concept enters into the judgment about this concept. Whatever is authentic in this concept also becomes so only under the perspective of something that is different from it. It is never pure in the concept itself. Otherwise the decision about it degenerates into hairsplitting. But at the same time, the essential element of a thing has its *fundamentum in re*. Over and against naïve usage, nominalism is in the wrong to the degree that it remains blind toward the objective element of meaning in words, which enters into the configurations of language and which changes there. This element of objectivity carries on an unresolved struggle with those acts that merely subjectively give meaning. The consciousness of this objective element in what is authentic was the impulse of Brentano's whole school, especially of Husserl, and also contributed to Heidegger's doctrine of authenticity. The essence of a thing is not anything that is arbitrarily made by subjective thought, is not a distilled unity of characteristics. In Heidegger this becomes the aura of the authentic: an element of the concept becomes the absolute concept. The phenomenologists pinpoint the *fundamentum in re* as the particularization of essence. This particularization becomes in itself thingly like a *res,* and can be called upon without regard to the subjective mediation of the concept. In his own argument Heidegger would like to escape Husserl's dualism, as well as the whole dispute of nominalism. He remains a tributary of Husserl's, however, in the short-circuited conclusion that imputes the authentic immediately to things, and thus turns the authentic into a special domain. Hence the substantivation of authenticity, its promotion to an existentiale, to a state of mind. By means of an alleged independence from thinking, the objective moment of that which is essential raises itself to something higher. Finally it becomes an absolute, the *summum bonum* over and against the relativity of the subject, while simultaneously it is presented as purely descriptive diagnosis in the manner of Scheler. Language nerves, which may be suspect to the authentics as something decadent revolt against that substantivation which thus befalls the authentics' favorite motto. "-Keit," "-ness," is the general concept for that which a thing is. It is always the substantivization of a characteristic. Thus industriousness is the substantivization of those characteristics that apply to all industrious people, and which they have in common. By contrast, however, "authenticity" names no authentic thing as a specific characteristic but remains formal, relative to a content which is by-passed in the word, if not indeed rejected in it—even when the word is used adjectivally. The word says nothing about what a thing is, but questions the extent to which the thing realizes what is posited by its concept. The thing stands in implicit opposition to what it merely seems to be. In any case the word would receive its meaning from the quality which it is a predicate of. But the suffix "-keit," "-ness," tempts one to believe that the word must already contain that content in itself. The mere category of relationship is fished out and in its turn exhibited as something concrete. By this logic the supreme would be that which is altogether what it is. The newly created Plato is more Platonic than the authentic one, who at least in his middle period attached its proper idea to everything, even to the humblest thing, and in no way confused the Good with the pure agreement between the thing and its idea. But in the name of contemporary authenticity even a torturer could put in all sorts of claims for compensation, to the extent that he was simply a true torturer.

The primacy of the concept over the thing is now, through the alliance of authenticity with mineness, pushed into mere detail. That detail is as artificial as was the *haecceitas* of Duns Scotus' late Scholasticism, which made a universal out of the indissolubility of the *Diesda* (*haecceitas*), and out of its not-being-universal —made it a paradigm of an ontologizing of the ontic.

The taboo concerning subjective reflection is useful to subjectivism: authenticity, in the traditional language of philosophy, would be identical with subjectivity as such. But in that way, unnoticed, subjectivity also becomes the judge of authenticity. Since it is denied any objective determination, authenticity is determined by the arbitrariness of the subject, which is authentic to itself. The jurisdictional claim of reason, which Husserl still asserted, falls away. Traces of reflection on such arbitrariness could still be found in *Sein und Zeit* in the concept of projection. That concept subsequently allowed the growth of all sorts of other ontological projections, most of them pleasantly watered down. With clever strategy the later Heidegger remodeled the concept. In the projection of the philosophizing subject something of the freedom of thought was preserved. The provocative aspect of an openly makeshift theory is no more embarrassing to Heidegger than is the suspicion of *hubris*. The armored man was so conscious of his unprotected places that he preferred to grasp at the most violent arrangement of arguments, rather than to call subjectivity by its name. He plays tactically with the subjective aspect of authenticity: for him, authenticity is no longer a logical element mediated by subjectivity but is something in the subject, in Dasein itself, something objectively discoverable. The observing subject prescribes whatever is authentic to the subject as observed: it prescribes the attitude toward death. This displacement robs the subject of its moment of freedom and spontaneity: it completely freezes, like the Heideggerian states of mind, into something like an attribute of the substance "existence." Hatred toward reifying psychology removes from the living that which would make them other than reified. Authenticity, which according to doctrine is absolutely unobjective, is made into an object. The reason for this is that authenticity is a manner of behavior that is ascribed to the being-a-subject of the subject, not to the subject as a relational factor. Thus it becomes a possibility that is prefixed to and foreordained for the subject, without the subject being able to do anything about it. Judgment is passed according to the logic of that joke about the coachman who is asked to explain why he beats his horse unmercifully, and who answers that after all the animal has taken on itself to become a horse, and therefore has to run. The category of authenticity, which was at first introduced for a descriptive purpose, and which flowed from the relatively innocent question about what is authentic in something, now turns into a mythically imposed fate. For all that distance from nature which marks an ontological structure that will rise again on the far side of the existent, this destiny functions as something merely naturelike. Jews are punished for being this destiny, both ontologically and naturalistically at the same time. The findings of Heidegger's existential analysis, according to which the subject is authentic insofar as it possesses itself, grant special praise to the person who is sovereignly at his own disposal; as though he were his own property: he has to have bearing, which is at the same time an internalization, and an apotheosis, of the principle of domination over nature. "Man is he, who he is, precisely in testifying to his own *Dasein*." [100] The testimony of his being-human, which constitutes "the existence of man," occurs "through the creation of a world and its ascent, as much as through the destruction of it and its decline. The testifying to humanity, and thus its authentic completion, occurs through the freedom of decision. This grasps necessity and puts itself under the commitment of a supreme order." [101] That very statement is nobly meant, quite in the spirit of the jargon, as when a noncommissioned officer bawls out the "weakness of the flesh." Outside of the tautology all we can see here is the imperative: pull yourself together. It is not for nothing that in Kierkegaard, the grandfather of all existential philosophy, right living is defined entirely in terms of decision. All his camp followers are in agreement on that, even the dialectical theologians and the French existentialists. Subjectivity, Dasein itself, is sought in the absolute disposal of the individual over himself, without regard to the fact that he is caught up in a determining objectivity. In Germany these determinations of objectivity are limited by the "sense of obligation to the command," as in the word-fetish "soldierly." This obligation is totally abstract and thus concretizes itself according to the power structure of the moment. In honor of all that, the existential ontologists and the philosophers of existence bury the hatchet of discord.

100. Heidegger, *Hölderlin und das Wesen der Dichtung* (Munich, 1937), p. 6.
101. *Ibid.*

Action of the warrior. The strength to make decisions under the most extreme conditions—life or death—comes from firmness in decision; comes from such firmness in unique situations which never recur in absolutely identical form. The fundamental traits of this kind of action are readiness for risks, along with a sense for what is possible; as well as artfulness and presence of mind. Rules can be formulated for this kind of action, but in its essence no rules will cover it completely; nor can this action be derived from rules. In the most extreme situations there appears both what I am authentically, and my potential.[102]

The speakers for existence move toward a mythology, even when they don't notice it. Self-possession, unlimited and narrowed by no hetcronomy, easily converges with freedom. Men would be reconciled with their essential definition if the time came when their defining limitations were no longer imposed on them. This would mean a happy reversal of the domination over nature. However, nothing is more unwanted by the philosophy and the jargon of authenticity. Apart from the right to come into one's own, self-control is hypostatized. No end to controls is sought; rather, the controls are carried over into the Being of Dasein. This is done according to the hoary custom of German Idealism. By that custom one should not speak of freedom without adding that it is identical with duty. Once one extrapolates from the words of empirical language what authentically is, as those words' authentic meaning, one sees that the merely existing world determines

102. Karl Jaspers, *Von der Wahrheit*, rev. ed. (Munich, 1958), p. 340. [Our translation. This work has been translated into English by J. T. Wilde, W. Klubach, W. Kimmel, *Truth and Symbol, from Von der Wahrheit* (New York, 1959).]

what on any specific occasion applies to those words; that world becomes the highest court of judgment over what should and should not be. Today, nevertheless, a thing is essentially only that which it is in the midst of the dominant evil; essence is something negative.

Paragraph 50 of *Sein und Zeit,* entitled: "*Preliminary Sketch of the Existential-onotological Structure of Death,*"—without the print even blushing—contains the sentence: "However, there is much that can impend for Dasein as Being-in-the-world." [103] Once somebody attributed to a local aphorist from Frankfurt the saying that "Whoever looks out of the window becomes aware of many things." Heidegger sketches his conception of authenticity itself, as Being toward death, on just this level. Such Being should be more than mortality disvalued as something thingly-empirical. But he also takes great care, for the sake of ontology, to separate this being from subjective reflection on death. Being oneself does not reside in an exceptional situation of the subject, freed from the They; it is no form of the subject's consciousness.[104] Authentic being toward death is no "thinking about death," [105] an activity which is displeasing to the monopolistic philosopher: "Needed, in our present world-crisis: less philosophy but more attention to thought; less literature, but more concern for the letter." [106] The attitude which he disapproves of

103. Heidegger, *Being and Time,* p. 294.
104. *Ibid.,* p. 168.
105. *Ibid.,* p. 305.
106. Heidegger, *Über den Humanismus* (Frankfurt a. M., 1949), p. 47.

"thinks about death," pondering over when and how this possibility may perhaps be actualized. Of course such brooding over death does not fully take away from it its character as a possibility. Indeed, it always gets brooded over as something that is coming; but in such brooding we weaken it by calculating how we are to have it at our disposal. As something possible, it is to show as little as possible of its possibility. On the other hand, if Being-towards-death has to disclose understandingly the possibility which we have characterized, and if it is to disclose it *as a possibility*, then in such Being-towards-death this possibility must not be weakened: it must be understood *as a possibility*, it must be cultivated *as a possibility*, and we must *put up with it as a possibility*, in the way we comport ourselves towards it.[107]

Reflection about death is anti-intellectually disparaged in the name of something allegedly deeper, and is replaced by "endurance," likewise a gesture of internal silence. We should add that the officer learns to die according to the tradition of the cadet corps; and yet to that end it is better if he does not trouble himself about that which, in his profession, is the most important thing—next to the killing of others. The fascist ideology had altogether to remove from consciousness that sacrifice which was proclaimed for the sake of German supremacy. The chance that such a sacrifice would reach the goal for which it was intended was from the outset too doubtful; it would never have been able to survive such a conscious inspection. In 1938 a National Socialist functionary wrote, in a polemical

107. Heidegger, *Being and Time*, pp. 305–6.

variation on a Social Democratic phrase; "Sacrifice will make us free." [108] Heidegger is at one with that. In the eighth printing of *What is Metaphysics?*, which appeared in 1960, he still retains—without any opportunistic mitigation—the following sentences:

> Sacrifice is the expenditure of human nature for the purpose of preserving the truth of Being for the existent. It is free from necessity because it rises from the abyss of freedom. In Sacrifice there arises the hidden thanks, which alone validates that grace—in the form of which Being has in thought turned itself over to the essence of man; that in his relation to Being he might take over the guarding of Being.[109]

Nevertheless, once authenticity can no longer be either the empirical condition of mortality nor the subjective relating to it, then it turns into grace. It turns, as it were, into a racial quality of inwardness, which man either has or does not have—a quality about which nothing further can be stated than that, tautologically, there is mere participation in it. Consequently, in his additional discussions of death Heidegger is irresistably driven on to tautological manners of speaking: "It [death] is the possibility of the impossibility of every way of comporting oneself toward anything, of every way of existing," [110] thus, perfectly simply, the possibility of no longer existing. One could well reply

108. Cf. Herbert Marcuse's critique in *Zeitschrift für Sozialforschung*, III (1938), 408.

109. Heidegger, *Was ist Metaphysik?* 8th ed. (Frankfurt a. M., 1960), p. 49. [Our translation. This work has been translated into English by R. F. C. Hull and Alan Crick, *What Is Metaphysics?* in *Existence and Being*, ed. Werner Brock (Chicago, 1949).]

110. Heidegger, *Being and Time*, p. 307.

at once that thinking about the states of being, or of being, is always tautological, because these states of being would be nothing other than themselves. Then, however, the mere recitation of words, with disregard for any thinking predicate, would have to liquidate thinking itself. The strategist guarded himself against drawing that conclusion; the philosopher drew it, however, in the matter at hand. For the sake of its own dignity, authenticity once more transforms theoretical lack, indeterminability, into the dictate of something that must be accepted without question. But what ought to be more than mere Dasein sucks its blood out of the merely existent, out of just that weakness which cannot be reduced to its pure concept, but which rather cleaves to the nonconceptual substratum. The pure tautology, which propagates the concept while at the same time refusing to define that concept—and which instead mechanically repeats the concept—is intelligence in the form of violence. The concern of the jargon, which always insists on having a concern, is to equate essence—"authenticity"—with the most brutal fact of all. Nevertheless this repetition compulsion betrays a failure: the violent mind's incapability of capturing what it should think about if it wanted to remain mind.

Violence inheres in the nucleus of Heidegger's philosophy, as it does in the form of his language. That violence lies in the constellation into which his philosophy moves self-preservation and death. The self-preserving principle threatens its subjects with death, as an *ultima ratio*, a final reason; and when this death is used as the very essence of that principle it means the theodicy of death. By no means in a simply untrue way. As Hegel sees it, the ego of idealism, which posits itself absolutely, and insists entirely on itself, turns into its own negation and resembles death:

> Therefore the only work and task of general freedom is death. It is death which has no inner ambience and fulfillment since it negates the unfulfilled center of the self, which is absolutely free. Thus it is the coldest and most platitudinous death, which has no more meaning than the cutting of a head of cabbage, or a drink of water.[111]

Hegel, disillusioned by the French Revolution, brought up against it all these things, as well as what touched on the violent essence of absolute selfness. For Heidegger those themes become not a motive for criticism of selfness but something unavoidable, therefore something which is a commandment. Violence is complicity with death, and not only superficially. There has always been a natural alliance between the views that everything, even one's self, should come to an end, and that on the other hand one should continue to follow his own limited interest, with a derogatory "What the hell!" Just as particularity, as a law of the whole, fulfills itself in its annihilation, so that blindness which is the subjective accompaniment of particularity has something nihilistic about it, for all its addiction to life. Ever since Spinoza, philosophy has been conscious, in various degrees of clarity, of the

111. Hegel, *Werke*, Vol. II: *Phänomenologie des Geistes*, p. 454. [Our translation. This work has been translated into English by J. B. Baillie, *The Phenomenology of Mind* (London and New York, 1961).]

identity between self and self-preservation. What asserts itself in self-preservation, the ego, is at the same time constituted by self-preservation; its identity constituted by its nonidentity. This still reverberates in the most extreme idealistic sublimation, the Kantian deduction of the categories. There the moments in which the identity of consciousness presents itself, and the unity of the consciousness which puts itself together from those moments, reciprocally condition one another, in opposition to the deductive intention—insofar as these and not other moments are absolutely given. The Kantian "I think" is the only abstract reference point in a process of holding out, and not something self-sufficient in relation to that process. To that extent it is already self as self-preservation. Of course Heidegger, in distinction from the abstract transcendental unity of Kant, forms his conception of selfness along lines related to Husserl's subject—a subject that, though phenomenologically reduced, appears in the "bracketing" of its empirical existence as a full subject with all its experiences.[112] But the concrete selfness meant by Heidegger is not to be had without the empirical, actual subject; it is no pure possibility of the ontic, but is itself always, at the same time, also ontic. Self is only intelligible in relation to this content, as it were. It is impossible to subtract the ontic and leave the ontological self as a remainder, or to preserve it as a structure of the ontic in general. It is senseless to assert, of something so thinned down, that it "exists authentically." To do so, Heidegger dogmatically and

112. Cf. Heidegger, *Being and Time*, pp. 168, 307. Also see above, pp. 116 ff.

vainly prolongs his conception of existence as something in opposition to identity; while without a break he continues the tradition of the doctrine of identity, with his implicit definition of the self through its own preservation. Against his intention, certainly, he falls back into the prehistory of subjectivity, instead of ontologically disclosing existence as a primal phenomenon; for it is no such thing. But he applies the most inwardly tautological relation of self to self-preservation as if it were, in Kantian terms, a synthetic judgment. It is as though self-preservation and selfhood defined themselves qualitatively through their antithesis, death, which is intertwined with the meaning of self-preservation.

As soon as Heidegger speaks out openly, his category of Dasein, as in the early period of bourgeois thought, is determined by its self-preserving principle, and through the existent's asserting of itself. In his own words: "The primary item in care is the 'ahead-of-itself,' and this means that in every case Dasein exists for the sake of itself." [113] He has no desire for this "for the sake of itself" to be understood naturalistically; yet the linguistic echo, as one aspect of the matter, cannot be erased; it cannot be eradicated from Heidegger's category of care, which according to him "is that which forms the totality of Dasein's structural whole." [114] According to his wish "the Being of the wholeness itself must be conceived as an existential phenomenon of a Dasein which is in each case one's own," [115] and ex-

113. Heidegger, *Being and Time*, p. 279.
114. *Ibid.*
115. *Ibid.*, p. 284.

istential orientation must be won from the particular Dasein in question. All that gives the ontological key-position, in the so-called analysis of existence, to self-preservation. But thereby the same position is also accorded to death. As a limit it not only determines Heidegger's conception of Dasein, but it coincides, in the course of the projecting of that conception, with the principle of abstract selfhood, which withdraws absolutely into itself, persevering in itself. "No one can take away another's dying," just as in Kantian idealism no ego can take away another's experiences, his "representations." The platitude gives mineness its excessive pathos. But death becomes the core of the self, as soon as it reduces itself completely to itself. Once self has emptied itself of all qualities, on the grounds that they are accidental-actual, then nothing is left but to pronounce that doubly pitiful truth, that the self has to die; for it is already dead. Hence the emphasis of that sentence, "Death *is*." For the ontology of *Sein und Zeit*, the irreplaceable quality of death turns into the essential character of subjectivity itself: this fact determines all the other determinations that lead up to the doctrine of authenticity, which has not only its norm but its ideal in death. Death becomes the essential element in Dasein.[116] Once thought recurs—as though to its ground—to the absolutely isolated individuality, then there remains nothing tangible for it except mortality; everything else derives only from the world, which for Heidegger, as for the idealists, is

116. *Ibid.* Cf. also Adolf Sternberger's 1932 criticism of *Being and Time,* in his dissertation *Der Verstandene Tod* (Grafenhainichen, 1933).

secondary. "With death, Dasein stands before itself in its ownmost potentiality-for-Being." [117] Death becomes the representative of God, for whom the Heidegger of *Sein und Zeit* felt himself to be too modern. Furthermore, it would seem to him too blasphemous to consider even the possibility of doing away with death; Being-unto-death, as an existentiale, is explicitly cut off from the possibility of any mere [*sic*] ontic doing away with it. Since death, as the existential horizon of Dasein, is considered absolute, it becomes the absolute in the form of an icon. There is here a regression to the cult of death; thus the jargon has from the beginning gotten along well with military matters. Now, as earlier, that answer is valid which Horkheimer gave to an enthusiastic female devotee of Heidegger's. She said that Heidegger had finally, at least, once again placed men before death; Horkheimer replied that Ludendorff had taken care of that much better. Death and Dasein are identified; death becomes pure identity, as in an eixstent which can absolutely not happen to any person other than oneself. The analysis of existence glides quickly over the most immediate and trivial aspect of the relation between death and Dasein, their simple nonidentity; the fact that death destroys Dasein truly negates it. Yet for all that, the analysis of existence does not disengage itself from triviality: "Death is the possibility of the absolute impossibility of Dasein." [118] Secondary school teachers speak thus in Wedekind's *Spring's Awakening*. The *characteristica universalis* of

117. Heidegger, *Being and Time*, p. 294.
118. *Ibid.*, pp. 294 ff.

Dasein, as in the Dasein of a mortal, takes the place of what must die. Thus death is manoeuvered into the position of the authentic; Dasein is "distinctive" [119] through the ontological, which it is anyway; and the analytical judgment becomes the precipitous philosopheme, the empty generality becomes the specific element in the concept—while to death, as "something distinctively impending," [120] a medal of honor is given. Formerly, the cultural-historical experience of the absence of ontological meaning inspired the movement of Heidegger's philosophizing; but now such absence, the blindness of the inescapable, becomes exactly that which is lacking to Heidegger's theory of death. In that way his thought brings out the hollowness which resounds from the jargon as soon as one knocks on it. Tautology and nihilism bind themselves into a holy alliance. Death is to be experienced only as something meaningless. That is alleged to be the meaning of the experience of death and, since death constitutes the essence of Dasein, such is also the meaning of Dasein. Hegel's metaphysics, which cannot be brought back again, and which had its positive absolute in the totality of negations, is here interiorized to a dimensionless point. In such a construction it is reduced to the Hegelian "fury of disappearance," [121] to the unmediated theodicy of annihilation.

Throughout history, identity thinking has been something deathly, something that devours everything. Identity is always virtually out for totality; the One as

119. Cf. p. 294.
120. *Ibid.*, p. 295.
121. Hegel, *Werke,* II, 453.

the indeterminate point, and the All-One—equally indeterminate, because it has no determination outside of itself—are themselves one. In Heidegger, as in idealism, that which tolerates nothing beyond itself is understood to be the whole. The least trace which went beyond such identity would be as unbearable as anyone who insists on his own individuality is to the fascist—no matter in what remote corner of the world. Therefore, not after all does Heidegger's ontology aspire to exclude every kind of facticity. Facticity would give the lie to the identity principle, would not be of the nature of the concept, which for the sake of its omnipotence would like precisely to gloss over the fact that it is a concept; dictators imprison those who call them dictators. Nevertheless, that identity, which strictly would be identical with nothing more than with itself, annihilates itself. If it no longer goes forth to an other, and if it is no longer an identity of something, then, as Hegel saw, it is nothing at all. Thus totality is also the moving principle of Heidegger's observations about death. They apply to wholeness, as that which is constitutively preestablished over its parts;[122] that wholeness which Heidegger's predecessor Scheler had already transplanted into metaphysics from a Gestalt psychology which was at first rather unpretentious. In prefascist Germany, wholeness was the motto of all the zealots who were opposed to the nineteenth century, which they looked on summarily as old-fashioned and done away with. The attack was par-

122. Occasionally Heidegger refers condescendingly to the concept of totality in other writers, but does so only to prove the superiority of his own concept.

ticularly directed against psychoanalysis; it stood for enlightenment in general. In those years, around the time of the first publication of *Sein und Zeit*, the doctrine of the precedence of the whole over its parts was the delight of all apologetic thinking—just as today it delights the adepts of the jargon. Heidegger directly and openly repeated that view of the then current habits of thought. That the task of philosophy is to sketch out the whole was for Heidegger as much an article of faith as the duty of system-making once was to the idealist:

> Thus arises the task of putting Dasein as a whole into our fore-having. This signifies, however, that we must first of all raise the question of this entity's potentiality-for-Being-a-whole. As long as Dasein is, there is in every case something still outstanding, which Dasein can be and will be. But to that which is thus outstanding, the "end" itself belongs. The "end" of Being-in-the-world is death. This end, which belongs to the potentiality-for-Being—that is to say, to existence—limits and determines in every case whatever totality is possible for Dasein.[123]

The thought model for this was in particular the "good Gestalt" of Gestalt theory: a forerunner of that understanding agreement between inner and outer that is to be destroyed by "consciousness as fate." In its turn the conception bears with it the marks of the same scientific division of labor against which its own anti-mechanistic attitude polemicizes. In that attitude the inwardness of individuals remains intact, without regard to society. Whether a rounded unity exists be-

123. Heidegger, *Being and Time*, p. 276.

tween subject and the surrounding world would be said to depend on the subject. It could only be wholeness insofar as it sets itself in opposition to reality, nonreflectingly. Therefore, accommodation, social compliance, is the goal even of a category like that of wholeness, which appears to be so anthropological or existential. An a priori partisanship toward the subject as such is exercised by the jargon in the name of man. Through this partisanship, attention is removed from the question of whether reality, with which men must be unmediately at one in order even to become wholes themselves, of whether this reality deserves being at one with; of whether in the end this reality, as heteronomous, does not deny them wholeness; of whether the wholeness ideal does not in fact contribute to their oppression and to the progressive atomization of those who are without power. As an expression of the whole situation the atomization of man is also the truth; the point would be to change the truth along with this situation, and not, within this situation, to wrest the truth away, and to charge it up to the forgetfulness of being, to the forgetfulness of those who recognize the truth. Heidegger felt a slight discomfort about an optimism that was secretly proud of having proven God in the laboratory; proud of having done so by the discovery of the Gestalt which is structured prior to all thinking preparation. But Heidegger's discomfort hid itself away in the rhetorical, and involuntarily comic, question of whether in view of death we can speak of wholeness. The thesis about immediately prediscovered, objective structuredness came just at the time when he needed it. With the help of a makeshift

thought construction, he brought together the obligation toward wholeness—accepted without question—
and the experience of our literally discontinuous life.
This was an experience needed by the expression of incorruptible earnestness. This is precisely the brokenness of existence, he says—following a Hegelian
schema which, alas, he stuck together almost mechanically. Presumably, death would make this brokenness
into a whole. Finitude, the infirmity of existence,
would enclose it as its very principle. Since negativity,
for all the brow-wrinkling, is taboo, Heidegger thinks
past his goal. If philosophy could define the structure
of Dasein at all, it would become for her two things at
once: broken and whole, identical with itself and not
identical—and that would of course drive one on to a
dialectic which broke through the projected ontology of
Dasein. But in Heidegger, thanks to that doctrine, it
becomes more evident than anywhere else that the
negative, as the essence, simply and undialectically
turns into the positive. He channeled into philosophy
the scientifically and psychologically circumscribed
doctrine of wholeness; the antithesis between the dispersed existent and Eleatically harmonic being is silently totted up to the debit of mechanistic thinking—
the primal scapegoat here being Aristotle. That this
thought should be "overcome"—as one of the most suspect expressions tirelessly continues to proclaim—was
not for a moment doubted even by Heidegger; such an
attitude created, for him, the double halo of the modern
and the supratemporal. The irrationalistic lackey-
language of the twenties prattled on about "body-soul
unity." The connection of existent elements to their

whole is supposed to be the meaning of people in real life—as it is in art; in the fashion of the *Jugendstil,* consolation is spread aesthetically over the harsh empirical world. To be sure, Heidegger's analysis of death carefully contents itself with applying the wholeness category to that of Dasein, instead of to individuals. The borrowing from the psychological theory of wholeness pays off after all. Its grammatical character is the renunciation of any causal argumentation, a renunciation which removes the alleged wholenesses from nature, and transfers them to the transcendence of Being. For this transcendence is really none at all; it does not, in the Kantian way, go beyond the possibility of experience, but rather behaves as though experience is itself unmediated, incontrovertible, aware of itself as if it were face to face with itself. A fictive bodily contact with phenomena aids this anti-intellectualism. The pride in controlling phenomena in their undisfigured state bases itself inexplicitly on a certain judgmental claim: that the world is divided up into thingly pieces through an unraveling thought-process, not through the structure of society. Still—in accord with the then reigning rules of the trade of philosophy —there is some talk of analysis; but this trade would already prefer to do no more analyzing.

The central chapter of *Sein und Zeit* treats "Dasein's possibility of Being-a-whole, and Being-towards-Death." [124] The question is raised—merely in a rhetorical fashion, as we can see at once—"whether this entity, as something existing, can ever become acces-

124. *Ibid.,* p. 278.

sible in its Being-a-whole." [125] It is obvious that a "possibility of this entity's Being-a-whole" [126] could contradict the self-preservation which has been ontologized into "care." Heidegger does not linger over the fact that, in his ontological determination of care as "that which forms the totality of Dasein's structural whole," [127] wholeness was already stipulated, through the transposition of the individual existent into Dasein—a wholeness which he then fussily proceeds to uncover. We can anticipate, as immanent in Heidegger, what he later announces with so much aplomb: that the fact of mortality does not a priori exclude the possibility that man's life should round itself out to a whole, as in the Biblical and epic conception. Heidegger may have been forced to the effort to ground existential wholeness by the undeniable fact that the life of individuals today does without wholeness.[128] Wholeness is supposed to survive despite historical experience. For this purpose the whole-being of the eixstent, toward which Heidegger's theory is heading —and out of which "concern" emerges in the jargon— the whole-being is distinguished, in the approved manner, from the merely cumulatively existent, *for which anything is still outstanding.*" [129] The latter is said to have "the same kind of Being as those which are ready-to-hand"; [130] to it is contrasted the totality raised into

125. *Ibid.*, p. 279.
126. *Ibid.*
127. *Ibid.*
128. Cf. the introduction to Benjamin, *Schriften I*, p. xxii.
129. Heidegger, *Being and Time*, p. 286.
130. *Ibid.*

an existential wholeness apart from the empirically individual life.

> The togetherness of an entity of the kind which Dasein is "in running its course" until that "course" has been completed, is not constituted by a "continuing" piecing-on of entities which, somehow and somewhere, are ready-to-hand already in their own right. That Dasein should *be* together only when its "not-yet" has been filled up is so far from the case that it is precisely then that Dasein is no longer. Any Dasein always exists in just such a manner that its "not-yet" belongs to it.[131]

That only applies to the extent that mortality is already thought together with the concept of Dasein—to the extent, that is, that Heidegger's philosophy is presupposed. For the ontologist, whole-being cannot be the unity of the whole content of real life but, qualitatively, must be a third thing; and thus unity will not be sought in life as something harmonious, articulated, and continuous in itself, but will be sought at that point which delimits life and annihilates it, along with its wholeness. As a nonexistent, or at least as an existent *sui generis*, outside life, this point is once again ontological. "But this lack-of-togetherness which belongs to such a mode of togetherness—this being-missing as still-outstanding—cannot by any means define ontologically that 'not-yet' which belongs to Dasein as its possible death. Dasein does not have all the kind of Being of something ready-to-hand-within-the world." [132] Removed from facticity, death becomes the ontological foundation of totality. Thus it becomes a

131. *Ibid.*, p. 287.
132. *Ibid.*, pp. 286 ff.

meaning-giving element in the midst of that fragmentation which, according to ontological topography, characterizes the atomized consciousness of the late industrial age. This is done according to a habit of thinking, unquestioned by Heidegger, which immediately equates a structural whole with its own meaning—even if it were the negation of all meaning. Thus death, the negation of Dasein, is decisively fitted out with the characteristics of Being.[133] Insofar as death is the ontological constituent of Dasein, death alone can give existence the dignity of totality: *"death as the end of Dasein, is Dasein's ownmost possibility—non-relational, certain and as such indefinite, not to be outstripped."* [134] Thus Heidegger gives a negative answer to his own starting question; the question which is only posed in order to be refuted:

So if one has given an ontologically inappropriate Interpretation of Dasein's "not-yet" as something still outstanding, any formal inference from this to Dasein's lack of totality will not be correct. *The phenomenon of the "not-yet" has been taken over from the "ahead-of-itself"; no more than the care-structure in general, can it serve as a higher court which would rule against the possibility of an existent Being-a-whole; indeed this "ahead-of-itself" is what first of all makes such a Being-towards-the-end possible.* The problem of the possible Being-a-whole of that entity which each of us is, is a correct one if care, as Dasein's basic state, is "connected" with death—the uttermost possibility for that entity." [135]

133. Cf. above pp. 142 ff.
134. Heidegger, *Being and Time*, p. 303.
135. *Ibid.*

147

Ontologically, existence becomes a totality by means of death, which disrupts Dasein ontically. Death, however, is authentic because it is removed from the They, which in turn is justified by the fact that there cannot be a proxy in death. Heidegger criticizes all thinkable real attitudes toward death as manifestations of the They. For, according to his own verdict, only the They speak of "death as a regularly occurring state of affairs." [136] Thus he singles out his authentic death as something that is extremely real and at the same time beyond all facticity. Since there cannot be a proxy in death it becomes as unconceptual as the pure *Diesda* (*haecceitas*). Its concept would precede it and would become its representative, as is the case in the relation of any concept to that which is its content. In the same breath, however, Heidegger slanders facticity, which alone allows him to speak of the impossibility of having a proxy in death. The reason for this lies in the fact that death as a general concept designates the death of all and not of each individual one. Death as event, factual death indeed, is not to be the authentic death. Thus ontological death is not all that terrible.

> In the publicness with which we are with one another in our everyday manner, death is "known" as a mishap which is constantly occurring—a "case of death." Someone or other "dies," be he neighbour or stranger [*Nächste oder Fernerstehende*]. People who are no acquaintances of ours are "dying" daily and hourly. "Death" is encountered as a well-known event occurring within-the-world. As such it remains in the inconspicuousness characteristic of what is encountered

136. *Ibid.,* p. 297.

in an everyday fashion. The "they" has already stowed away . . . an interpretation for this event. It talks of it . . . expressly or else in a way which is mostly inhibited, as if to say, "One of these days one will die too, in the end; but right now it has nothing to do with us." [137]

In his eagerness to distinguish between death as an event and death as something authentic, Heidegger does not turn his back on sophisms.

The analysis of the phrase "one dies" reveals unambiguously the kind of Being which belongs to everyday Being-towards-death. In such a way of talking, death is understood as an indefinite something which, above all, must duly arrive from somewhere or other, but which is proximally *not yet present-at-hand* for oneself, and is therefore no threat. The expression "one dies" spreads abroad the opinion that what gets reached, as it were, by death, is the "they." In Dasein's public way of interpreting, it is said that "one dies," because everyone else and oneself can talk himself into saying that "in no case is it I myself," for this "one" is *the* "*nobody*." [138]

To say that death affects the They already presupposes, as it were, Heidegger's hypostasis of the existentiales, the dark side of which is always the They. Such an interpretation neglects and falsifies the truth in that talk, threadbare as it may be. This truth is the fact that death is a general determination which comprehends the alter ego as well as one's own. If someone says, "one dies," he includes himself euphemis-

137. *Ibid.*, pp. 296–97.
138. *Ibid.*, p. 297.

149

tically at best. However, the adjournment of death, criticized by Heidegger, takes place: the one who speaks is actually still allowed to live—otherwise he wouldn't speak. Besides, such argumentation, set in motion by Heidegger, necessarily takes place in the sphere of nonsense; and in turn gives the lie to authenticity, which is to crystallize itself in this sphere as if it were the philosopher's stone. If anything fits the They, then it is such a pro and contra. The "occurrence" which "belongs to nobody in particular" [139] and which is not highly valued by Heidegger, definitely belongs to someone, according to the usage of language. It belongs to him who dies. Only a solipstistic philosophy could acknowledge an ontological priority to "my" death over and against any other. Even emotionally, someone else's death is easier to experience than one's own. The Schopenhauer of the fourth book of the *World as Will and Idea* did not miss this fact:

> In him, too, as in the unthinking animal, there prevails a sense of security as a permanent state, a security which springs from the innermost conscious-that man is nature, that he himself is the world. Because of this security no man is noticeably bothered by the thought of a certain and never distant death; but everyone continues to live as if he were to live eternally. This goes so far, that one could say that no one actually has a living conviction about the certainty of his death. Otherwise there could not be such a great difference between his mood and that of the convicted criminal. Each man, however, recognizes this certainty theoretically and in abstracto but like any other truth, which is not usable in

139. *Ibid.*

practice, puts it aside without taking it into his living consciousness.[140]

For Heidegger the They becomes a cloudy mixture of elements which are merely ideological products of the exchange relationship. The mixture contains the *idola fori* of condolence speeches and obituaries, as well as that humanity which does not identify the other, but identifies itself with the other, breaks through the circle of abstract selfness and recognizes the latter in its mediation. The general condemnation of that sphere, which philosophy dubiously enough called intersubjectivity, hopes to overcome reified consciousness by means of a primary subject that is supposedly untouched by reification. Yet in truth such a subject is as little something immediate and primary as is anything else. Heidegger's key sentences run in the following manner:

> Death is Dasein's *ownmost* possibility. Being towards this possibility discloses to Dasein its *ownmost* potentiality-for-Being, in which its very Being is the issue. Here it can become manifest to Dasein that, in this distinctive possibility of its own self it has been wrenched away from the "they." This means that in anticipation any Dasein can have wrenched itself away from the "they" already.[141]

Death becomes the essence of the realm of mortality. This occurs in opposition to the immediate, which is characterized by the fact that it is there. Death thus

140. Arthur Schopenhauer, *Sämtliche Werke in fünf Bänden*, Grossherzog Wilhelm Ernst-Ausgabe (Leipzig, n.d.), Vol. I: *Die Welt als Wille und Vorstellung*, p. 376.
141. Heidegger, *Being and Time*, p. 307.

becomes something that is artificially beyond the existent. Saved from the They it becomes the latter's sublime counterpart; it becomes the authentic. Authenticity is death. The loneliness of the individual in death, the fact that his "non-relatedness singles out Dasein unto itself," [142] becomes the substratum of selfness. This attitude of total self-sufficiency becomes the extreme confirmation of the self; it becomes an Ur-image of defiance in self-abnegation.As a matter of fact, abstract selfness *in extremis* is that grinding of the teeth which says nothing but I, I, I. Thus it is characterized by the same nothingness that the self becomes in death. But Heidegger's language blows up this negative element into that which is substantial. This, then, is the content from which was taken the stenciled model for the formal procedure of the jargon. Involuntarily, Heidegger's doctrine becomes an exegesis of the futile joke: Only death is free and that costs your life. He is smitten with death as that which is supposed to be absolutely removed from the universal exchange relationship. Yet he does not realize that he remains caught up in the same fatal cycle as the exchange relationship which he sublimates into the They. Insofar as death is absolutely alien to the subject, it is the model of all reification. Only ideology praises it as a cure for exchange. This ideology debases exchange into the more despairing form of eternity, instead of getting rid of proper exchange by letting it fulfil itself properly. For Heidegger, Dasein is not sufficiently able to justify itself, because of its shameful historical form.

142. *Ibid.*

It redeems itself only in its destruction, which it itself is to be. The highest maxim of such an attitude results in saying that "it is so," that one has to obey—or, in positivistic terms, that one has to adapt oneself. This is the pathetic commandment that he must obey that which is. It is not even really obeying, for in any case Dasein does not have a choice. Precisely for this reason death is so ontological in regard to Dasein. If one were to call nonideological a kind of thinking which reduces ideology to the zero limit, then one would have to say that Heidegger's thinking is nonideological. But his operation once again becomes ideology because of his claim that he recovers the meaning of Dasein. This happens after the fashion of today's talk about the loss of ideology—talk which tramples down ideology but would like to trample down the truth.

By saying *"the 'they' does not permit us the courage in the face of death,"* [143] Heidegger actually lays bare certain elements of ideology, such as the attempt to integrate death into just that societal immanence which has no power over death. A similar development can be seen in Evelyn Waugh's parody *The Loved One.* Some of Heidegger's formulas come very close to the mechanism of sublimating death. "But temptation, tranquillization, and alienation are distinguishing marks of the kind of Being called *'falling.'* As falling, everyday Being-towards-death is a constant *fleeing in the face of death.*" [144] Alienation, however, designates a social relationship, even if it is the relationship to death. Man and the institutions of piety reproduce

143. *Ibid.,* p. 298.
144. *Ibid.*

commercially the unconscious will to forget what one has to fear. Fundamental ontology and its nomenclature are not necessary for insights like the following:

> In this manner the "they" provides a *constant tranquillization about death.* At bottom, however, this is a tranquillization not only for him who is "dying" but just as much for those who "console" him. And even in the case of a demise, the public is still not to have its own tranquillity upset by such an event, or be disturbed in the carefreeness with which it concerns itself. Indeed the dying of Others is seen often enough as a social inconvenience, if not even a downright tactlessness, against which the public is to be guarded.[145]

In the same manner Ibsen's assessor Brack already concluded, about Hedda Gabler's suicide, "One doesn't do that sort of thing." Heidegger, who does not want to have anything to do with psychology, has seen through the reactionary nature of the integration of death. He has himself done this in a psychological fashion. The message is coded in *Sein und Zeit:*

> But in thus falling and fleeing *in the face* of death, Dasein's everydayness attests that the very "they" itself already has the definite character of *Being-towards-death,* even when it is not explicitly engaged in "thinking about death." *Even in average everydayness, this ownmost potentiality-for-Being which is non-relational and not to be outstripped, is constantly an issue for Dasein. This is the case when its concern is merely in the mode of an untroubled indifference towards the uttermost possibility of existence.*[146]

145. *Ibid.,* pp. 298 ff.
146. *Ibid.,* pp. 298–99.

In spite of that, he does not go far enough. Heidegger cannot make us feel and respect the despair embodied in that cramped "Enjoy life" and in that stupid commonplace, "One will die sometime, but not quite yet" [147]—a commonplace which he rightly despises. The commonplace represses our despair. The protestation against the sublimating of death would have its place in a criticism of liberal ideology. That criticism would proceed to remind us of the naturalness which is denied by culture. For in domination culture itself propagates this naturalness. It does it by means of that which mistakes itself for the antithesis to nature. Instead of this, Heidegger does the same thing as fascism; he defends the more brutal form of Being, negative as it may be. It is possible to think of a social state in which men would no longer have to sublimate death and might be able to experience it in another form than fear. To experience death in fear is a mark of the crude natural state that Heidegger's doctrine has eternalized in supranaturalistic terms. Death is sublimated because of a blinded drive for self-preservation; its terror is part of the sublimation. In a life that is no longer disfigured, that no longer prohibits, in a life that would no longer cheat men out of their dues—in such a life men would probably no longer have to hope, in vain, that this life would after all give them what it had so far refused. For the same reason they would not have to fear so greatly that they would lose this life, no matter how deeply this fear had been ingrained in them. From the fact that men sublimate death, one

147. *Ibid.*, p. 299.

cannot conclude that death is itself the authentic. Heidegger is least of all in a position to do this, as he is careful not to attribute authenticity to people who do not sublimate death.

By means of a kind of philosophical Freudian slip, Heidegger himself defines the ontologizing of death insofar as death, in its certainty, is qualitatively superior to other phenomena. "We have already characterized the everyday state-of-mind which consists in an air of superiority with regard to the certain 'fact' of death—a superiority which is 'anxiously' concerned while seemingly free from anxiety. In this state-of-mind, everydayness acknowledges a 'higher' certainty than one which is only empirical." [148] The "higher," in spite of the quotation marks, has the proving force of a confession: theory sanctions death. The partisan of authenticity commits the same sin of which he accuses the *minores gentes,* the lesser people, of the They. By means of the authenticity of death as he flees from it. Whatever announces itself as "higher" than mere empirical certainty, in this attitude, falsely cleanses death from its misery and stench—from being an animalistic kicking of the bucket. This cleansing occurs in the same manner as a Wagnerian love- or salvation-death. All this is similar to the integration of death into hygiene, of which Heidegger accuses the inauthentic. By means of that which is kept silent in the high stylization of death, Heidegger becomes an accomplice of what is horrible in death. Even in the cynical materialism of the dissection room, this horribleness is

148. *Ibid.,* p. 302.

recognized more honestly and denounced more strongly than in the tirades of ontology. The latter's kernel is nothing but the supraempirical certainty that death is something that has been existentially preordained to Dasein. Purity untouched by experience plays over into that which it once was unmetaphorically: purity untouched by dirt. But by no understanding can death be said to be pure. Neither is it anything apodictic. Otherwise, all the salvation promises of religion would simply be forgetful of Being. However, they are by no means needed. Some lower organisms do not die in the same sense as the higher, individuated ones. Thus, in light of our potential, and growing, control over organic processes, we cannot do away a fortiori with the thought that death might be eliminated. Such an elimination of death may be highly improbable; yet it can be thought of, and according to existential ontology that should be impossible. The affirmation of the ontological dignity of death, however, is already reduced to nothing by the possibility that something can change it ontically—according to Heidegger's language. Insofar as Heidegger cuts off these hopes at what inquisitors probably call the root, the authentic one speaks for all—for all those who join, as soon as they hear of this possibility, in the refrain that nothing would be worse than the disappearance of death. It seems legitimate to assume that those are the adepts of the jargon. The eagerness toward the eternity of death prolongs the continuing use of death as a threat. On a political level death advertises the necessity of wars. Kant, who subsumed immortality under the Ideas, did not let himself fall to those depths in which nothing else flourishes but the affirmation of what is all too familiar. If Heidegger had made the transition from the inorganic to the organic, the existential horizon of death would have been thoroughly changed. His philosophy, and everything that floats with it, down to the last sewers of German faith unto being, could nowhere be more vulnerable than in this transition. That understanding with the existent which motivates the elevation of the existent to being thrives on the complicity with death. In the metaphysics of death there comes to a head all that evil to which bourgeois society has physically condemned itself, by means of its own process of development.

The doctrine of anticipation, which is the authentic Being unto death, the "possibility of taking the *whole* of Dasein, in advance . . . in an existentiell manner; that is to say, it includes the possibility of existing as a whole potentiality-for-Being," [149] underhandedly becomes a mode of behavior. Thus it becomes what Being-unto-death did not want to be and yet has to be if anything more than a tautology is thereby to be uttered. Although nothing is said about the difference of this mode of behavior from the fact that one has to die, this behavior is expected to acquire dignity by accepting such a necessity speechlessly and without reflection.

> Anticipation, however, unlike inauthentic Being-towards-death, does not evade the fact that death is not to be outstripped; instead, anticipation frees itself *for* accepting this. When, by anticipation, one becomes free

149. *Ibid.*, p. 309.

for one's own death, one is liberated from one's lostness in those possibilities which may accidentally thrust themselves upon one; and one is liberated in such a way that for the first time one can authentically understand and choose among the factical possibilities lying ahead of that possibility which is not to be outstripped. Anticipation discloses to existence that its uttermost possibility lies in giving itself up, and thus it shatters all one's tenaciousness to whatever existence one has reached.[150]

Only rarely do Heidegger's words contain as much truth as these last ones. Man's thinking about himself as nature would simultaneously mean a critical reflection on the principle of self-preservation: the true life would be one that does not insist on "tenaciousness to whatever existence one has reached." In his doctrine of death, however, Heidegger extrapolates such a mode of behavior from Dasein, as the positive meaning of Dasein. He affirms self-abnegation as an instance of the self, and he spoils the insight he has gained. Resignation becomes an obstinacy which turns the dissolution of the self into an inflexibly stoic positing of the self. By means of relentless identification, of the dissolution of the self with the self, self becomes the absolute positing of the negative principle. All the categories that Heidegger then uses to explain Being unto death are linked with obstinacy: the possibility of death is supposed to be "put up with." [151] That which should be different from domination and inflexibility raises domination to its extreme. The subject is never so authentic for Heidegger as in that

150. *Ibid.*
151. *Ibid.*, p. 305.

holding out in which it endures an extreme of pain, following the example of the ego. Even the elements with which he contrasts the stiffening of the self carry linguistic traces of the domination of the self: he calls it a "breaking." [152] In the same way that Dasein-subject is actually identified with death, Being-unto-death becomes subject, pure will. Ontological decisiveness must not ask what it dies for. The last word is spoken by a selfness that remains unmoved. "This distinctive and authentic disclosedness, which is attested in Dasein itself by its conscience—*this reticent self-projection upon one's ownmost Being-guilty, in which one is ready for anxiety*—we call 'resoluteness.'" [153] The real ideological life would be this: the courage to be afraid only when this courage would no longer have to dissipate into all that which has to be feared.

The jargon of authenticity is ideology as language, without any consideration of specific content. It asserts meaning with the gesture of that dignity by which Heidegger would like to dress up death. Dignity, too, is of an idealistic nature. There was a time when the subject thought itself a small divinity, as well as a lawgiving authority, sovereign in the consciousness of its own freedom. Such motifs have been extirpated from the dignity of the Heideggerian tone:

> In what other way, however, could a humanity ever find the way to the primal form of thanking, if the favor of Being did not grant man the nobility of poverty by means of the open possibility of relating to Being? For only that nobility of poverty conceals in it the freedom

152. *Ibid.*, pp. 308–9.
153. *Ibid.*, p. 343.

of sacrifice which is the treasure of its essence. Sacrifice means farewell from the existent on the way to the preservation of the favor of Being. Nevertheless, sacrifice can be prepared in the working and effecting [*Leisten*] within the existent, yet such action can never fulfill the sacrifice. The fulfillment of sacrifice stems from the urgency out of which the action of every historical man rises—essential thinking, too, is an action—by means of which he preserves the achieved Dasein for the preservation of the dignity of Being. This urgency is the equanimity which does not allow itself to be tempted, in its hidden readiness for the farewell nature of any sacrifice. Sacrifice is at home in the essence of the event. In the form of an event being claims man for the truth of Being. For this reason sacrifice does not allow for any calculation. Calculation always reduces sacrifice to a purpose or purposelessness, whether such purposes are set high or low. Such a calculation disfigures the nature of sacrifice. The desire for purposes distorts the clarity of the courage for sacrifice, which is marked by an awe which readily fears; and which has taken upon itself to live in the neighborhood of that which is indestructible.[154]

In these sentences dignity certainly plays a role as the dignity of being, and not of men. Yet the solemnity of these sentences differs from the solemnity of secularized burials only through its enthusiasm for irrational sacrifice. Combat pilots may have spoken in exactly this way when they returned from a city just destroyed by bombs and drank champagne to the health of those who did not return. Dignity was never anything more than the attitude of self-preservation aspiring to be more than that. The creature mimes the cre-

154. Heidegger, *Was ist Metaphysik?*, p. 45.

ator. In dignity a feudal category is mediated which bourgeois society presents posthumously for the legitimation of its hierarchy. Bourgeois society always has had the tendency to swindle—as is clearly shown by delegated officials on festive occasions, when they appear in all the fastidiousness of prescribed demeanor. Heidegger's dignity is once again the shadow of such a borrowed ideology. The subject who founds his dignity at least on the Pythagorean claim—questionable as it may be—that he is a good citizen of a good country, is replaced. His dignity gives way to that respect which the subject can claim by the mere fact that, like all others, he has to die. In this respect Heidegger involuntarily proves to be a democrat. Identification with that which is inevitable remains the only consolation of this philosophy of consolation: it is the last identity. The worn-out principle of the self-positing of the ego, which proudly holds out in preserving its life at the cost of the others, is given a higher value by means of the death which extinguishes it. What was once the portal to eternal life has been closed for Heideggerian philosophy. Instead, this philosophy pays homage to the power and dimension of the portal. That which is empty becomes an *arcanum:* the mystery of being permanently in ecstasy over some numinous thing which is preserved in silence. In the case of taciturn people, it is too often impossible to tell whether—as they would like one to believe—the depth of their inwardness shudders at the sight of anything profane, or whether their coldness has as little to say to anything as anything has to say to it. The rest is piety, and in the more humane instance this rest is the helplessly surging feeling of people who have lost someone they loved. In the worst instance it is the convention that sanctions death by means of the thought of divine will and divine grace—even after theology has pined away. That is what is being exploited by language, and what becomes the schema of the jargon of authenticity. Its dignified mannerism is a reactionary response toward the secularization of death. Language wants to grasp what is escaping, without believing it or naming it. Naked death becomes the meaning of such talk—a meaning that otherwise it would have only in something transcendent. The falseness of giving meaning, nothingness as something, is what creates the linguistic mendacity. Thus the *Jugendstil* wanted to give meaning, out of itself, to a meaninglessly experienced life, by means of abstract negation. Its chimerical manifesto was engraved into Nietzsche's new tablets. Nothing of the kind can any longer be voluntarily elicited from late bourgeois Dasein. That is why meaning is thrown into death. The dramas of the later Ibsen closed with the freely committed self-destruction of life that is caught up in the labyrinth of conventions. This self-destruction was a necessarily violent consequence of the action, as if it were its fulfillment. Yet it was already close to the purifying death of agnostic cremation. But the dramatic form could not resolve the vain nature of such action. The subjectively consoling meaning of self-destruction remained objectively without consolation. The last word is spoken by tragic irony. The weaker the individual becomes, from a societal perspective, the less can he become calmly aware of his own impotence. He has to puff himself up into selfness, in the way the futility of this selfness sets itself up as what is authentic, as Being. There is an involuntary parody of Heidegger, by an author who brought forth, one after another, books with titles like *Encounter with Nothingness* and *Encounter with Being*. But this author cannot be blamed for his parody. It has to be blamed on its model, which thinks itself superior to such depravities. Heidegger, too, only encounters nothingness with a higher propaedeutic of Being. The Heideggerian tone of voice is indeed prophecied in Schiller's discussion of dignity. Schiller sees it as something secluding oneself within oneself, or as a kind of securing.

If we have many occasions to observe the affected grace in the theatre and in the ballroom, there is also often occasion for studying the affected dignity in the cabinet of ministers and in the study-rooms of men of science (notably at universities). True dignity is content to prevent the domination of the affections, to keep the instinct within just limits, but there only where it pretends to be master in the involuntary movements; false dignity regulates with an iron sceptre even the voluntary movements, it oppresses the moral movements, which were sacred to true dignity, as well as the sensual movements, and destroys all the mimic play of the features by which the soul gleams forth upon the face. It arms itself not only against rebel nature, but against submissive nature, and ridiculously seeks its greatness in subjecting nature to its yoke, or, if this does not succeed, in hiding it. As if it had vowed hatred to all that is called nature, it swathes the body in long, heavy-plaited garments, which hide the human structure; it paralyses the limbs in surcharging them with vain ornaments, and goes even the length of cutting the hair to replace this gift of nature by an artificial production.

True dignity does not blush for nature, but only for brute nature; it always has an open and frank air; feeling gleams in its look; calm and serenity of mind is legible upon the brow in eloquent traits. False gravity, on the contrary, places its dignity in the lines of its visage; it is close, mysterious, and guards its features with the care of an actor; all the muscles of the face are tormented, all natural and true expression disappears, and the entire man is like a sealed letter.

But false dignity is not always wrong to keep the mimic play of its features under sharp discipline, because it might betray more than would be desired, a precaution true dignity has not to consider. True dignity wishes only to rule, not to conceal nature; in false dignity, on the contrary, nature rules the more powerfully within because it is controlled outwardly.[155]

The Kantian, who believed in his master's disjunction between price and dignity, could still see this as something to be desired. Because of that, however, the great writer fell short of the full insight to which he came close. This is the insight that dignity contains the form of its decadence within itself. The fact can be observed when intellectuals become accomplices of that power which they don't have and which they should resist. The Kantian dignity finally disintegrates into the jargon of authenticity. With it goes that humanity which has its basic nature not in self-reflection but in its difference from a suppressed animality.

155. Friedrich von Schiller, *Sämtliche Werke* (Stuttgart, 1818), "Über Anmut und Würde," Vol. VIII, pt. I, pp. 96 f. [English edition edited by N. H. Dole, *The Works of Schiller* (Boston, 1902), "On Grace and Dignity," pp. 231 ff.]